LOW FODMAP

COOKBOOK

365 DAYS OF GUT FRIENDLY RECIPES TO HEAL YOUR IBS FOREVER | 28-DAY MEAL PLAN FOR BEGINNERS

BY DEBBY HAYES

TABLE OF CONTENTS

INTRODUCTION

You might not even know you have it! At first, I thought I just had a "sensitive system." But as time went on, and I increasingly had to give up foods I loved and (even worse) had to give up going out to dinner – since who wants to be severely flatulent during the movie?! – I got tired of how IBS (irritable bowel syndrome) cramped both my stomach and my lifestyle.

The symptoms of IBS gut distress are debilitating and often painful. Like me, most individuals with IBS suffer from frequent stomach pain that feels like abdominal cramping. This pain is often also accompanied by alternating periods of diarrhea with constipation, gas/flatulence, and mild-to-severe bloating.

I tried six different medications prescribed for the disorder, and it took 3 years of experimenting with each of them before I found an alternative solution. Unfortunately, I found that all these medications worsened either the constipation or the diarrhea from which I consistently suffered. I now know it was all triggered by certain ingredients in food!.

Luckily, I finally heard about the Low-FODMAP diet. This diet has been successful in relieving almost all symptoms in 86% of people with IBS who have tried it.

So, I decided to try the diet for myself. Now that I have used the Low-FODMAP system to determine my true food sensitivities, I can enjoy eating again! I only have to avoid a short-list of certain types of foods containing certain ingredients.

The result: I've been completely symptom-free for 4 years now.

It's for this reason that I've created the recipes in this book. My hope is to help you make it through the first phase of the diet (i.e., the elimination phase) more deliciously. These recipes are all delicious, easy to make, and are – especially – quick to create for those of you with busy lifestyles.

WITH WHAT KINDS OF CONDITIONS CAN A LOW-FODMAP DIET HELP?

A low-FODMAP diet has been proven, as I stated earlier, to help relieve most of the symptoms associated with IBS. However, a low-FODMAP diet has also been found to be helpful for people with other distressing gut conditions and types of Functional Gastrointestinal Disorders, including:

- Small Intestinal Bacterial Overgrowth (SIBO)
- Depression
- Fibromyalgia
- Eczema
- Rheumatoid Arthritis
- Chron's
- Ulcerative Colitis
- Inflammatory Bowel Disease (IBD)

You might be wondering why rheumatoid arthritis and eczema have been listed here, but when you consider that most of our immune system lies in our gut and skin specialists everywhere are discovering the link between the skin and gut microbiome, you can see why!

WHAT THE HECK ARE FODMAPS ANYWAY?

FODMAP stands for Fermentable, Oligo, Di-Mono-Saccharides And Polyols. These three strange-sounding compounds are, basically, fermentable carbohydrates found in food that we now know ferment in the gut and small intestine, rather than in the large intestine where they should ferment to nourish the good bacteria.

This fermentation process that takes place outside of the large intestine is what causes the bloating, gas, diarrhea/constipation, and discomfort associated with IBS.

SO WHAT FOODS ARE HIGH IN FODMAPS?

The list containing high-FODMAP foods is quite long, so please bear with me.

GRAINS
The following are all high-FODMAP grains (many people find that by simply eliminating wheat from their diet, they are able to eliminate most to all IBS symptoms):

- Barley
- Couscous
- Farro
- Rye
- Semolina
- Wheat

FRUITS
Fructose, especially high-fructose, is a problem for people with IBS. The following fruits are all high in FODMAPs and fructose:

- Apples
- Apricots
- Blackberries
- Cherries
- Grapefruit
- Mango
- Nectarines
- Peaches
- Pears
- Plums
- Pomegranates
- Watermelon

VEGETABLES
Vegetables contain short-chain carbohydrates and sugars. The following vegetables are high in FODMAPs:

- Artichokes
- Asparagus
- Beets
- Brussel sprouts
- Cauliflower
- Celery

- Garlic
- Leeks
- Onion
- Scallions (the white parts)
- Shallots
- Mushrooms
- Okra
- Peas
- Snow peas
- Sugar snap peas

BEANS AND LEGUMES

The following beans and legumes are high in FODMAPs:

- Baked beans
- Black-eyed peas
- Butter beans
- Chickpeas
- Kidney beans
- Lentils
- Lima beans
- Soybeans
- Split peas

DAIRY AND DAIRY SUBSTITUTES

The following dairy products and substitutes are high in FODMAPs:

- Buttermilk
- Cream
- Cottage cheese
- Ice cream
- Margarine
- Milk (from cows, goats, or sheep)
- Soft cheeses (e.g., mascarpone and Swiss cheese)
- Yogurt (regular and Greek)
- Oat milk
- Soy milk

SWEETENERS

Most sweeteners are particularly high in FODMAPs, and many people find that by simply eliminating these from their diet, they are able to eliminate their IBS symptoms. Some such sweeteners include:

- Agave
- Fructose
- High fructose corn syrup
- Honey
- Isomalt
- Maltitol
- Mannitol
- Sorbitol
- Xylitol

Now, before I get to what low-FODMAP foods you'll be eating, let me first give a quick summary on this three-phase diet. The main thing to remember is that you only have to eat completely low-FODMAP foods during Phase I of the diet. In Phase II you will start reintroducing high-FODMAP foods, one by one. Then in Phase III, all foods you tolerate well can be introduced back into your diet – for good! Now that you understand the structure, I'll list the low-FODMAP foods as I describe Phase I.

HOW AND WHY IT WORKS

Researchers currently believe that most individuals have food sensitivities, with possibly several working together. These sensitivities, in turn, are what cause the gut problems associated with IBS.

What the FODMAP diet does is, little by little, help individuals to identify and then eliminate foods – vegetables, certain sweeteners, certain foods containing these sweeteners, etc. – from their diet. For example, I read somewhere that xylitol gum helped improve gum and dental health, and I really enjoyed being able to chew gum and know I was improving the health of my teeth. However, it turned out that xylitol was causing me a lot of gut distress, and since I was chewing it after every meal...well, there you go!! Thank God I figured that one out!

The low-FODMAP diet can similarly help you to, one by one, identify the kinds of foods and compounds in your own diet that are causing you to suffer IBS symptoms. And – here's the beauty of it – you might only have to eliminate two or three foods from your diet!

For me, the problem was chiefly sweeteners in food. I love coffee and chewing gum after I've had some coffee. By simply eliminating the gum, which contained these sweeteners, I was able to relieve, I'd say, around 80% of my problem.

The other problem for me were that I love eating Italian food and lots of salads. Specifically, I used a lot of mushrooms in my homemade tomato sauces and salads, not to mention the stuffed mushroom caps that I served with steaks, the canned mushroom soup I used in most of my vegetable casseroles, and the pizza I ordered from local pizzerias. Problem was, with all these mushrooms, I was ingesting a lot of a food for which I have a super-sensitivity.

How did I figure this out? By using a food diary. And you're going to need one too – preferably a big one! Let me explain why.

WHY YOU NEED A GOOD FOOD DIARY FOR THE LOW-FODMAP DIET

You're going to be documenting your life for weeks of eating and you'll want space to make notes. I used huge, well-bound spirals and attached 2 weeks' worth of calendar-looking squares on them. I also left plenty of room on the sides of these squares to take notes – you might want a square for breakfast, lunch, and dinner. When I identified a food for which I had a sensitivity, I drew a big arrow to the side in red and put, "EUREKA! Don't eat this anymore, Deb!"

HOW THE DIET WORKS: THE THREE PHASES OF THE LOW-FODMAP DIET

As I mentioned earlier, this diet moves through three distinct phases. Just a note: the longer you do the elimination phase, by the way, the more reliable the results will be from the other two phases.

For me, since I had really been relishing the heck out of sweeteners in virtually every packaged food and sweetened beverage I drank (since the age of 13!) I did a 6-week elimination phase.

PHASE I: ELIMINATION PHASE (2-6 WEEKS)

This first phase is when you will only eat your low-FODMAP foods. This means you eliminate all high-FODMAP foods from your diet (see the lists of foods presented earlier) and only eat foods from the following lists.

It won't be as bad as you think, and the recipes in this book will help you create delicious meals with these low FODMAP foods!

I initially thought I'd have to give up my beloved milk and coffee creamer. But, instead, I just went organic and lactose-free on both of these and discovered a whole new level of deliciousness that can be found in milk and coffee!

LOW-FODMAP FOODS

(for a far more extensive list, including condiments, dips, cooking ingredients, specific lettuces, greens, spices, etc., please visit IBS Diets.org allowable low FODMAP food list.)

DAIRY AND DAIRY SUBSTITUTES
- Almond milk
- Feta cheese
- Hard cheeses (not soft, shredded, or Baby Swiss), like cheddar, parmesan
- Lactose-free milk

FRUITS
- Bananas (unripe)
- Blueberries
- Coconut
- Guava (ripe)
- Lemons
- Limes
- Oranges
- Papaya
- Pineapple
- Plantain (peeled)
- Raspberries

- Strawberries

SWEETENERS (YES, YOU CAN STILL SWEETEN THINGS UP!)

NOTE: I'm listing only those recommended sweeteners that are known to be safe:

- White, Raw and Brown sugar
- Maple syrup
- Stevia

VEGETABLES

- Bok choy (delicious and so nutritious – this is the time to try it if you haven't yet!)
- Bell peppers (all colors)
- Carrots
- Cucumbers
- Aubergine
- Green beans
- Kale
- Lettuce (green leaf or iceberg)
- Potatoes
- Spinach
- Tomatoes
- Zucchini

LENTILS AND LEGUMES

It's a pretty short list, but you'll find you'll be able to reintroduce some beans into the diet that don't irritate the gut at all after the reintroduction phase!

- Canned chickpeas
- Canned lentils
- Peanut butter
- Firm tofu (unflavored/plain)
- Tempeh (unflavored/plain)

NUTS AND SEEDS

- Almonds
- Brazil nuts
- Hazelnuts
- Macadamia nuts
- Peanuts
- Pecans
- Pine nuts
- Seeds (chia, dill, hemp, poppy, pumpkin, sesame, sunflower)
- Walnuts

FISH AND SEAFOOD

- Canned tuna
- Fresh, wild-caught fish (cod, haddock, plaice, trout, tuna)

MEATS

- Bacon
- Beef
- Ham (not processed – check for high-FODMAP ingredients)
- Lamb
- Pork

POULTRY

- Chicken
- Turkey
- Duck

OILS

- Avocado oil
- Coconut oil
- Olive oil
- Sesame oil

ARE THERE LOW-FODMAP OPTIONS OF YOUR FAVORITE HIGH-FODMAP FOODS? YES!!

Foods can switch from low- to high-FODMAP based on portion size. So, many of the vegetables and fruits on the high-FODMAP list are not really high-FODMAPs if you eat them in smaller portion sizes. But, you have to stick to some really small portion sizes.

Luckily, I have found, sometimes, that just a taste of, for example, raisins is quite enough to keep me from craving them all the time. Similarly, celery is critical to making tuna salad taste good, but you really don't need very much of it.

Another good example is almonds. You can't eat 20 almonds without throwing yourself into high-FODMAP territory. But, you can eat 10 almonds, which qualifies as a low-FODMAP addition to any salad, casserole, cereal, or snack. Again, 10 almonds is quite enough to quash a craving, or add crunch to a salad.

Here are typically high-FODMAP foods that become low-FODMAP when eaten in smaller portion sizes:

	High-FODMAP Portion Size	Low-FODMAP Portion Size
Apples (Granny Smith/Pink Lady)	> 8 tsp.	< 8 tsp.
Avocado	> 0.7 oz or ⅛ avo	< 0.7 oz or ⅛ avo
Blueberries	1 cup	¼ cup
Celery	>2" stalk	< 2" stalk
Corn on the Cob	> half an ear	< half an ear
Raisins	> 1 tbsp.	< 1 tbsp.
Savoy Cabbage	> ½ cup	< ½ cup
Snow Peas	> 5 pods	< 5 pods

So, to reiterate, you can eat some of the foods you think you must avoid completely – but just a taste or two.

You do, however, want to completely avoid these foods during the elimination phase to be completely accurate in spotting your food sensitivities!

Again, you are allowed to consume only low-FODMAP foods from the presented list during the elimination phase. You should notice a lot of relief from discomfort during this phase! In fact, most individuals report feeling better in just 7 days.

In this book, I have given you 4 weeks' worth of yummy food ideas and recipes. Select your favorites for weeks 5 and 6, should you want a six-week elimination phase.

PHASE II: THE REINTRODUCTION PHASE (6-10 WEEKS)

This second phase takes quite a while, and you'll want to really take your time with this to properly sort out your diet.

What you do in this phase is to continue to eat low-FODMAP foods while reintroducing high-FODMAP foods, one at a time, to chart any food sensitivities. You want to wait 3-4 days in between each food reintroduction to avoid any crossover effect.

What I did was to break the food groups up, rather than to move my way systematically through all the meats, then cheeses, then nuts, seeds, etc. For example, I'd try xylitol on a Monday, then, if I had a reaction, I'd wait 4-5 days before trying another food from a different food group, so as to avoid any crossover effects. Then I'd pick something with a lower risk of reaction, like asparagus, for my next high-FODMAP food to try. If I had no reaction, then 3 days later, I could try another high-risk food, like whole milk. In this way, I managed to work my way through all the high-FODMAP foods.

In the end, I only had to give up sweeteners, mushrooms, and buttermilk – not a hard diet to live with at all!

PHASE III: THE INTEGRATION PHASE

Phase III is all about creating your own personalized diet based on the foods you need to eliminate and learning to live without them.

For me, that meant going Italian without mushrooms. For you, it may mean that you find that there are several sweeteners working together to create your gut distress. Your journey will then be about learning to read food labels, as many of these kinds of sweeteners are found in foods as far-reaching as macaroni and cheese to canned soup.

You may also find that a whole foods diet, which completely eliminates processed foods, could be key for you in completely eradicating all gut distress.

Are you ready to discover the most delicious ways to make it through the elimination phase? Are you looking forward to discovering a whole new way of eating that will make sure you never feel deprived, yet removes all gut distress, diarrhea, constipation, and stomach pain?

Just turn the page to my breakfast, lunch, dinner, and snack recipes!

You'll never even know you're on a diet of any kind. And, you'll get freedom from pain, discomfort, and a house-bound/bathroom-bound lifestyle.

I wish you all the luck in the world with your new gut-distress-free lifestyle!

28 Day Meal Plan

B. Breakfast   **L.** Lunch   **D.** Dinner

DAY 1	DAY 2	DAY 3	DAY 4	DAY 5
B. Blueberry & Banana Flapjacks **L.** Homemade Burrito 2-Ways **D.** Wild Rice & Ginger Cod	**B.** Eggy Breakfast Tators **L.** Italian-Herb Pasta Salad **D.** Low-FODMAP Chicken Curry	**B.** Nutty Buckwheat-Oats with Fruit **L.** Beef & Zucchini Stir-Fry **D.** Italian-Style Pasta & Shrimp	**B.** Chive-Topped Smoked Salmon Toast **L.** Nutty Chicken & Mustard Salad **D.** Cilantro Pork & Stir-Fry Vegetables	**B.** Spicy Poached Italian-Style Eggs **L.** Bok Choy Tuna Salad **D.** Potato Curry in Coconut Milk

DAY 6	DAY 7	DAY 8	DAY 9	DAY 10
B. Fluffy Vanilla Buckwheat Griddle Cakes **L.** Bok Choy Tuna Salad **D.** Greek-Style Lamb Skewers	**B.** Hearty Turmeric Beef Toast **L.** Thai-Garden Rice Toss **D.** Cheesy Chicken on Toasted Wraps	**B.** Italian Crustless Quiche **L.** Maki Roll Shrimp Salad **D.** Cheesy Spinach-Stuffed Filet Mignon	**B.** Banana French Toast **L.** Moroccan Chicken & Orange Sauce **D.** Spicy Fried Shrimp & Broccoli	**B.** Nourishing Basmati Rice Gruel **L.** Hearty Beef & Mustard Salad **D.** One-Pan Turkey & Corn Bread

DAY 11	DAY 12	DAY 13	DAY 14	DAY 15
B. Poached Eggs in Dutch Sauce **L.** Low-FODMAP Toasted Tuna Sandwich **D.** Spicy Jamaican Shredded Pork	**B.** Fruity Yogurt Protein-Packed Breakfast **L.** Nutty Chicken & Mustard Salad **D.** Zesty Pan-Fried Snapper Fillets	**B.** Cheesy Country Omelet **L.** Blue Cheese Bacon Salad **D.** One-Pan fried Tilapia with Olives	**B.** Spicy Poached Italian-Style Eggs **L.** Maple & Lime Glazed Salmon **D.** Quick Italian Herb Chicken	**B.** Anytime Crispy Waffles **L.** French Salad with Mustard Dressing **D.** Zesty Asian-Style Chicken

DAY 16	DAY 17	DAY 18	DAY 19	DAY 20
B. Heat-Up Breakfast Wraps **L.** Hearty Vegetarian Lettuce Bowls **D.** Spicy Ham and Shrimp Jambalaya	**B.** Zesty Granadilla Crêpes **L.** Nutty Gluten-Free Pasta Salad **D.** Tangy Ground Turkey Buns	**B.** Halaby Pepper & Avocado Toast **L.** Hearty Beef & Mustard Salad **D.** Mexican-Style Fish Wraps	**B.** Chive-Topped Smoked Salmon Toast **L.** Thai-Garden Rice Toss **D.** Sweet & Spicy Glazed Chicken	**B.** Zesty Blueberry Microwave Muffin **L.** Brown Rice & Vegetable Bowl **D.** Autumn Pasta with Crispy Bacon

DAY 21	DAY 22	DAY 23	DAY 24	DAY 25
B. Italian Crustless Quiche **L.** Caramelized Autumn Salad **D.** Italian-Style Beef Casserole	**B.** Nutty Buckwheat-Oats with Fruit **L.** Italian-Herb Pasta Salad **D.** Balsamic-glazed Salmon & Swiss Chard	**B.** Anytime Crispy Waffles **L.** Hearty Vegetarian Lettuce Bowls **D.** Decadent low-FODMAP Lasagna	**B.** Eggy Breakfast Tators **L.** Bok Choy Tuna Salad **D.** Greek-Style Lamb Skewers	**B.** Poached Eggs in Dutch Sauce **L.** Homemade Burrito 2-Ways **D.** Wild Rice & Ginger Cod

DAY 26	DAY 27	DAY 28		
B. Hearty Turmeric Beef Toast **L.** Maki Roll Shrimp Salad **D.** Cheesy Baked Beef Wraps	**B.** Nourishing Basmati Rice Gruel **L.** Butternut Salad with Pomegranate Seeds **D.** Sweet & Spicy Glazed Chicken	**B.** Heat-Up Breakfast Wraps **L.** Beef & Zucchini Stir-Fry **D.** One-Pan Turkey & Corn Bread		

BREAKFAST

NUTTY BUCKWHEAT-OATS WITH FRUIT

COOK TIME: 10-15 MINS | MAKES: 4 SERVINGS

INGREDIENTS:

- ¼ tsp. kosher salt
- 4 cups water
- ½ cup rolled oats
- 1 cup cracked buckwheat cereal
- Ground cinnamon
- Ground nutmeg
- 1 tsp. butter
- Macadamia or rice milk
- 1 tbsp. dried cranberries or raisins (limit: 1 tbsp. per serving)
- ½ cup blueberries or unripe bananas
- 1 tbsp. toasted almonds (limit 1: tbsp. per serving)
- 2 tbsp. toasted pecans or walnuts (limit: 2 tbsp. per serving)

DIRECTIONS:

1. In a small pot over medium heat, whisk the salt into the water before stirring in the oats and cereal. Gently stir the oats and cereal until the mixture begins to boil. Once the mixture is boiling, place the lid on the pot and allow it to cook undisturbed for about 10 minutes, or until the mixture has reached the desired consistency.

2. While the oat-cereal mixture is cooking, place the remaining ingredients in small bowls and set aside.

3. Spoon the cooked mixture into bowls and stir in any of the toppings as desired. If adding spices, stir these in before adding any other ingredients. A splash of milk or butter will yield a creamer bowl of oats. Enjoy!

(Tips: An additional sweetener, such as a tiny amount of maple syrup, may be added, but I suggest that you try the recipe without this addition and opt for the fruits and nuts on their own. The type of buckwheat recommended in this recipe is Bob's Red Mill Organic Creamy Buckwheat Hot Cereal. The nutritional value of the rolled oats remains the same as whole-uncracked, but will cook much quicker.)

EGGY BREAKFAST TATORS

COOK TIME: 15 MINS | MAKES: 4 SERVINGS

INGREDIENTS:

- 4 free-range eggs
- Kosher salt
- 1 small red yam, peeled and cubed into bite-sized pieces
- 2 large russet potatoes, peeled and cubed into bite-sized pieces
- 2 tbsp. olive oil
- 3 tbsp. chopped chives
- 1 large red bell pepper, seeded and diced
- ½ tsp. saffron
- Freshly-ground black pepper
- ½ avocado, sliced (optional)

DIRECTIONS:

1. Place the eggs in a small pot with just enough water to cover them and bring to a boil over medium heat. Once the water is boiling, allow the eggs to cook for 3 minutes. After the 3 minutes, place the eggs in a bowl of ice water and set aside.

2. Combine the red yam and potatoes into a pot. Generously sprinkle the vegetables with salt before covering them with water and bringing the water to a rolling boil. Once the water is boiling, lower the heat and cook the vegetables until fork-tender (approx. 5-7 minutes). Pour the cooked vegetables into a colander over the sink and allow them to drain while you prepare the rest of the dish.

3. Heat the oil in a large frying pan over medium-high heat. When the oil is hot, toss in the chives, bell pepper, and saffron. Stir until the peppers are just beginning to soften. Toss in the cooked yams and potatoes, stirring for an additional 4-5 minutes, or until the veggies are nice and crisp. Set the pan aside and cover with a lid to seal in the heat.

4. Remove the shells and chop the eggs into thin slices. Plate the cooked potatoes and garnish with the chopped egg before seasoning with salt and pepper to taste.

5. Serve with the avocado on top if desired.

(Tips: The eggs can be left out entirely to comply with any allergies or food restrictions. Try adding some fresh arugula before serving for a fresher taste. This dish can be stored in the fridge for up to 1 week, or eaten as a healthy snack.)

ZESTY GRANADILLA CRÊPES

COOK TIME: 35 MINS | MAKES: 4-5 SERVINGS

INGREDIENTS:

- ¾ cups fine white sugar
- 2 large egg yolks
- 2 large eggs (whole)
- ⅓ cup lemon juice
- 4 tsp. grated lemon peel
- 2 tbsp. butter

For Crêpes:
- ½ tsp. kosher salt
- 1 cup gluten-free, all-purpose flour
- ¾ cups water

- ½ cup almond milk (extra if needed)
- 2 tbsp. melted butter
- 2 large eggs (whole)
- ½ tsp. pure vanilla extract
- Sunflower oil for frying

Toppings:
- Pulp from 4 granadillas
- Icing sugar for dusting

DIRECTIONS:

1. In a small pot, whisk together the sugar, egg yolks, and eggs until you have a properly combined mixture (approx. 3-4 minutes). Transfer the pot to low heat and whisk in the lemon juice, lemon peel, and butter. Once the butter has melted, turn up the heat and whisk continuously for 5-7 minutes, or until the mixture thickens. When tiny bubbles appear on the surface, remove the curd from the heat and set aside.

2. In a large bowl, whisk together the salt and flour before beating in the water, almond milk, butter, and eggs until the batter is completely lump-free. Place the batter in the fridge for 30 minutes before using, or up to 12 hours. Once your batter has chilled, make sure that it is a proper pouring consistency. If the batter is too thick, you can add a little almond milk at a time to thin it out.

3. Lightly coat a large skillet with baking spray before coating the bottom of the pan with a thin layer of sunflower oil. Heat the oil over medium heat before carefully pouring ¼ cup of the batter into the pan. Gently lift the pan and tilt it from side to side until the batter has evened out. Fry for 2 minutes before carefully lifting an edge of the crêpe. If the bottom is nicely browned, flip and fry the other side for an additional 1 minute. Transfer the cooked crêpe to a plate.

4. Repeat the process with the remaining batter, adding oil as needed, until all the crêpes are done.

5. Build your crêpes with a dollop of granadilla pulp drizzled with the cooled lemon curd. Garnish with a sprinkle of icing sugar and serve.

(Tips: The lemon curd can be refrigerated for up to 2 weeks in an airtight container. Substitute the butter with a dairy-free option if necessary.)

BLUEBERRY & BANANA FLAPJACKS

COOK TIME: 20 MINS | MAKES: 2-3 SERVINGS

INGREDIENTS:

- 2 small, unripe bananas
- 2 large, free-range eggs
- 1 tbsp. light brown sugar
- ¼ tsp. ground nutmeg
- ½ tsp. ground cinnamon
- ½ tsp. pure vanilla extract
- ⅓ tsp. kosher salt
- ¼ tsp. baking powder

- 2 tbsp. gluten-free, all-purpose flour
- 3 tbsp. butter for cooking (more if needed)
- 6 tbsp. coconut yogurt
- 10 large blueberries
- Icing sugar for dusting

DIRECTIONS:

1. Place the pealed bananas in a large bowl and use a potato masher to mash them into a pulp. Beat in the eggs. Whisk in the brown sugar, nutmeg, cinnamon, vanilla extract, kosher salt, baking powder, and all-purpose flour until you have a lump-free batter.

2. Allow your skillet to heat to over medium heat before adding 1 tbsp. of butter. Once the butter has melted, scoop in 1 or 2 tbsp. batter onto the pan, depending on how big you would like your flapjacks to be. (NOTE: Do not tilt the pan as you would do with pancakes; rather, allow the batter to spread itself out.)

3. The flapjack should be ready to flip after 2-3 minutes, or when tiny bubbles begin to appear on the top of the batter. Flip the flapjack and cook the other side for an additional 1-2 minutes, or until both sides have been lightly browned.

4. Try to maintain a constant heat throughout as you cook the rest of the batter. Add more butter between flapjacks, as needed.

5. Once you've cooked all your flapjacks, divide them between your plates and dollop each one with 1 tbsp. coconut yogurt. Arrange the blueberries over the yogurt and finish with a sprinkling of icing sugar. Enjoy!

(Tips: Replace the butter with a dairy-free option, as required. Bananas should always be unripe when eaten on a FODMAP diet.)

ITALIAN CRUSTLESS QUICHE

COOK TIME: 1 HOUR 30 MINS | MAKES: 10-12 SERVINGS

INGREDIENTS:

- 2 tbsp. garlic-infused olive oil
- ¼ cup spring onions, chopped, whites discarded
- 2 medium zucchinis, trimmed and chopped into ¼" rounds
- 2 medium summer squashes, trimmed and chopped into ¼" rounds
- 5 different colored bell peppers, seeded and chopped into ¼" strips
- Himalayan salt
- 1 lb. russet potatoes, peeled and chopped into 1" cubes
- 8 large, free-range eggs
- 1 tsp. crushed thyme
- Freshly ground black pepper
- 9 oz. hard yellow Swiss cheese, shredded
- 8 oz. chèvre cheese, shredded

DIRECTIONS:

1. Set your oven to preheat at 325°F – ensure that the wire baking rack is placed in the middle of the oven. Prepare your dish by coating a 9" cake pan with baking spray.

2. Heat a large, thick bottomed pan over medium heat before adding the oil and spring onions. Fry the spring onions until the onions are tender (approx. 5 minutes). Stir in the zucchinis, summer squashes, and bell peppers until everything is covered with oil. Allow the vegetables to fry for 15-20 minutes with the lid on the pan, or until the vegetables are tender but still crisp. Stir every few minutes.

3. Transfer the cooked vegetables to a colander set over the sink and allow all the juices to drain. You can use the back of a wooden spoon to press out any excess juices. Leave the vegetables to drain while you prepare the rest of the dish.

4. Boil the potatoes in a pot of salted water until fork-tender. Pour the potatoes into a separate colander over the sink and allow them to drain.

5. In a large bowl, whisk together the eggs and thyme. Season to taste with salt and pepper. Toss in the potatoes and vegetables before adding the cheeses. Stir until everything is properly combined.

6. Pour your egg mixture into the baking pan. Gently shake the pan to evenly distribute the ingredients. Place the pan onto the rack in the middle of the oven. Allow the quiche to cook for about 1 hour, or until the center is no longer runny and the edges are slightly browned. Keep an eye on the quiche and cover it with tin foil if you see that the edges are browning too fast.

7. Allow the quiche to rest for 5-10 minutes outside the oven before serving.

(Tip: The quiche can be served hot or cold.)

ON-THE-GO NUTTY OATS

COOK TIME: 0 MINS| MAKES: 1 SERVING

INGREDIENTS:

- ¼ cup toasted almonds, chopped
- 1 tbsp. low-FODMAP protein powder
- ½ tsp. ground cinnamon
- 1 ½ tsp. chia seeds
- 1 tbsp. pure maple syrup
- ½ cup rolled oats
- ½ cup almond milk

DIRECTIONS:

1. Place all the ingredients in a large bowl and stir them until properly combined. Spoon the mixture into a glass jar and seal with a lid. Refrigerate overnight.

2. Grab the oats to eat cold, on the go. Alternatively, simply pop the jar into the microwave for a few minutes before eating.

(Tips: You can prepare numerous jars in advance and keep them in the fridge for up to 5 days. Add some blueberries for a fruitier taste.)

NOURISHING BASMATI RICE GRUEL

COOK TIME: 20 MINS | MAKES: 1 SERVING

INGREDIENTS:

- 2 cups warm water
- 1 tsp. salt
- 1 cup basmati rice
- 2 tsp. ground cinnamon
- ⅓ tsp. ground nutmeg
- 2 tbsp. pure maple syrup
- 1 can unsweetened coconut milk

DIRECTIONS:

1. Bring the water to a rolling boil in a medium pot before reducing the heat and stirring in the salt and rice. Allow the rice to simmer for 1 minute.

2. Stir in the cinnamon, nutmeg, pure maple syrup, and unsweetened coconut milk. Cook the rice with the lid on the pot for roughly 20 minutes, stirring every few minutes. Remove the pot from the stove when the rice is tender and the water has been absorbed.

3. Serve straight away, as this dish does not keep well!

(Tips: If you are cutting carbs or avoiding sugar altogether, simply replace the pure maple syrup with a sweetener of your choice, like Yacon syrup. If you struggle with your digestion, try soaking the rice overnight before cooking.)

POACHED EGGS IN DUTCH SAUCE

COOK TIME: 10 MINS | MAKES: 2 SERVINGS

INGREDIENTS:

- 1 tbsp. white vinegar
- 4 large, free-range eggs (whole)
- ⅛ tsp. fine white sugar
- 2 large egg yolks
- 1 ½ tsp. lemon juice
- Kosher salt
- Freshly ground black pepper
- 2 tbsp. melted butter
- Buttered, low-FODMAP toast
- Shredded iceberg lettuce

DIRECTIONS:

1. Add 1 ¼" water to a deep skillet and bring to boil. Once the water is boiling, whisk in the vinegar and reduce the heat until the water is gently simmering.

2. Crack each of the four eggs into a small bowl (NOTE: You can crack the eggs into a fine-mesh sieve to get rid of any loose white pieces if you want a neater egg).

3. Whisk the water in the skillet until the water is swirling in a vortex on its own. Carefully pour one egg into the swirling water and cook for about 2 minutes. Remove the cooked egg using a slotted spoon and allow the egg to drain on a paper towel while you repeat the process with the remaining 3 eggs. Swirl the water with each additional egg.

4. In a large bowl, whisk together the sugar, egg yolks, lemon juice, and a pinch of salt and pepper to taste. Add the melted butter and whisk.

5. Microwave the sauce for 1 minute, stopping and whisking every 10 seconds, until you have a thick sauce.

6. Place the buttered toast on plates and top with the lettuce and poached eggs. Dollop the sauce on top of the eggs and season to taste with extra salt and pepper if desired.

(Tip: Replace the butter with a dairy-free substitute to fit any dietary requirements.)

FLUFFY VANILLA BUCKWHEAT GRIDDLE CAKES

COOK TIME: 12 MINS | MAKES: 2-3 SERVINGS

INGREDIENTS:

- ½ tsp. kosher salt
- 1 tbsp. brown sugar
- 1 ¼ tbsp. baking powder
- ½ cup buckwheat flour
- ¾ cups rice flour
- 4 tbsp. butter (more for cooking)
- 1 cup + 2 tbsp. lactose free milk (more if needed)

- 1 tsp. pure vanilla extract
- 2 large, free-range eggs
- Blueberries (optional)
- Pure maple syrup (optional)

DIRECTIONS:

1. In a medium bowl, whisk together the salt, sugar, baking powder, buckwheat flour, and rice flour.

2. Heat a small pot over medium heat, add the butter and swirl until melted. Transfer the pot to a wooden chopping board and whisk in the milk and vanilla. The milk should have cooled the butter to just under warm, if not, wait a few minutes before whisking in the eggs.

3. Carefully beat the milk mixture into the flour. Beat the batter for a few minutes to incorporate as much air as possible. The batter should be thick, but not so thick that it can't be poured. Add extra milk if needed.

4. Heat a griddle pan over medium-low heat before adding ½ tsp. butter. When the pan is nice and hot and the butter has melted, ladle ¼ cup of the batter onto the hot griddle. You can use the back of the ladle to spread the batter out a little if you like a bigger griddle cake. The griddle cake is ready to be flipped when tiny bubbles poke through the surface of the batter and the edges are lightly browned. Use a spatula to flip the cake and cook the other side for 1-2 minutes until golden brown. Transfer the griddle cake to a plate and repeat the process with the remaining batter, adding butter as needed to the pan.

5. The griddle cakes are best served hot with 1 tbsp. pure maple syrup per cake and topped with blueberries.

(Tips: Buckwheat is gluten-free, wheat-free, and low-FODMAP, despite the name containing 'wheat'. Substitute the butter for a dairy-free option if needed.)

ZESTY BLUEBERRY MICROWAVE MUFFIN

COOK TIME: 1-2 MINS | MAKES: 1 MUFFIN

INGREDIENTS:

- 1 free-range egg
- 3 tbsp. brown sugar
- 3 tbsp. lemon juice
- $1/3$ tsp. lemon zest
- ¼ tsp. pure vanilla extract

- 2 tbsp. + 1 tsp. sunflower oil
- 5 tbsp. low-FODMAP, gluten-free pancake mix
- 3 tbsp. blueberries
- ¼ tsp. ground cinnamon

DIRECTIONS:

1. In a medium bowl, whisk the egg until it is light and fluffy. Spoon 2 tbsp. of the egg into a microwave-safe mug and keep the rest of the egg in the bowl or refrigerate for another dish. Use a fork to whisk the sugar into your mug. Gradually drizzle in the lemon juice and zest while whisking. Add the vanilla and sunflower oil. Whisk until everything is properly combined.

2. Beat in the pancake mix until everything is properly combined. Gently stir in the blueberries, making sure that none of them are peaking out of the batter, as this will cause them to burst inside the microwave and make a mess. Sprinkle the cinnamon over the top of the batter.

3. Place the mug in the microwave and cook for 1 ½-3 minutes or until the muffin has risen nicely in the mug.

(Tips: This recipe should not overflow in the microwave, so you do not have to be concerned. Frozen blueberries should be rinsed under lukewarm water until they have defrosted, so as to prevent them from liquidizing during cooking.)

NUTTY BANANA SMOOTHIE

COOK TIME: 0 MINS | MAKES: 2 SERVINGS

INGREDIENTS:

- 2 tbsp. almond butter
- 1 tsp. maple syrup
- ½ cup coconut milk

- 1 frozen, unripe banana
- 1 cup lactose free milk
- $1/3$ tsp. pure vanilla extract

DIRECTIONS:

1. Place all of the ingredients in a food processor and pulse on high until you have a lump-free smoothie.

2. Pour the smoothie into a glass and enjoy.

(Tips: The almond butter and almond milk can be substituted with extra coconut water to accommodate any tree nut allergies. While this smoothie can be stored in the fridge for 24 hours in an airtight container, it is best enjoyed straight away.)

FRUITY YOGURT PROTEIN-PACKED BREAKFAST

COOK TIME: 0 MINS | MAKES: 1 SERVING

INGREDIENTS:

- 1 tbsp. gluten-free, low-FODMAP protein powder
- 1 tbsp. almond butter
- $1/3$ unripe banana
- ½ cup mixed berries (blueberries, raspberries, and strawberries)
- 1 ½ tsp. pure maple syrup
- ½ cup unsweetened coconut yogurt
- 1 tsp. chia seeds
- 1 tbsp. toasted coconut
- 2 tbsp. rolled oats

DIRECTIONS:

1. Place the protein powder, almond butter, unripe banana, mixed berries, pure maple syrup, and coconut yogurt in a food processor and blend on the highest setting for about 1 minute, or until you have a smooth fruity yogurt.

2. Pour the fruity yogurt into a bowl and sprinkle with chia seeds, toasted coconut, and rolled oats.

(Tip: You may use berry substitutions, but blackberries are not low-FODMAP and should be avoided as much as possible.)

CHIVE-TOPPED SMOKED SALMON TOAST

COOK TIME:0 MINS | MAKES: 1 SERVING

INGREDIENTS:

- ½ tsp. dried chives
- ¼ tsp. garlic-infused oil
- 2 tbsp. lactose-free cream cheese
- 1 slice low-FODMAP or gluten-free bread
- ¾ oz. plain smoked salmon
- Freshly ground black pepper
- Kosher salt
- Chopped fresh dill

DIRECTIONS:

1. In a small bowl, whisk together the dried chives, garlic-infused oil, and cream cheese.

2. Toast the bread.

3. Spread the cream cheese mixture over the toast. Add the salmon. Season to taste with pepper and salt before garnishing with the fresh dill. Enjoy!

(Tip: Cream cheese is not low-FODMAP in large amounts, so do not exceed the 2 tbsp. limit.)

HALABY PEPPER & AVOCADO TOAST

COOK TIME: 0 MINS | MAKES: 1 SERVING

INGREDIENTS:

- 1 English cucumber, thinly sliced
- Kosher salt
- Black pepper
- ¼ tsp. paprika
- ¼ tsp. Halaby pepper
- ¼ small avocado
- ½ tsp. lime juice
- Gluten-free bread

DIRECTIONS:

1. In a medium bowl, toss the cucumber slices in with a pinch each of salt, pepper, paprika, and Halaby pepper.

2. In a separate bowl, mash the quarter avocado with a fork and season to taste with salt and pepper before stirring in the lime juice.

3. Toast the bread. Spread the mashed avocado over the toast in an even layer. Arrange the spiced cucumber slices over the avocado and serve.

(Tip: This recipe is best eaten straight away, as avocado does not keep well.)

ANYTIME CRISPY WAFFLES

COOK TIME: 20 MINS | MAKES: 4-6 SERVINGS

INGREDIENTS:

- 1 tsp. kosher salt
- 1 tbsp. + 1 tsp. baking powder
- 2 tbsp. brown sugar
- 2 cups gluten-free, all-purpose flour
- ½ cup butter, cubed
- 1 ½ cups almond milk
- 1 tsp. pure vanilla extract
- 2 large, free-range eggs
- Pure maple syrup for serving

DIRECTIONS:

1. Set the oven to preheat at 200°F to keep the waffles warm and then preheat your waffle iron. (NOTE: Preheating a waffle iron will depend on the brand, so be sure to check the packaging for instructions.)

2. In a large bowl, whisk together the salt, baking powder, brown sugar, and all-purpose flour. Reserve for later.

3. In a small pot over medium-low heat, whisk the butter and milk together until the butter has melted. Transfer the pot to a wooden chopping board and allow the milk and butter to cool until it is just under warm. Whisk in the vanilla and eggs. Create a hole in the center of the flour mixture and pour the milk into the center, whisking until everything is just combined – do not over mix.

4. Once your waffle iron is hot, lightly coat the inside with baking spray before pouring some of the batter into the mold. Make sure that the batter touches the sides in an even layer but does not overflow. Cook the waffle for 4-5 minutes, or until golden brown. Place the waffles in the oven while you cook the rest of the batter.

5. Serve with a drizzle of pure maple syrup.

(Tips: Although maple syrup is low-FODMAP in small amounts, try not to exceed 1 tbsp. per waffle.)

CHEESY COUNTRY OMELET

COOK TIME: 25 MINS | MAKES: 4 SERVINGS

INGREDIENTS:

- Himalayan salt
- 2 russet potatoes, peeled and chopped into small cubes
- 2 tbsp. garlic-infused oil
- 2 bunches Swiss chard
- 1 red bell pepper, seeded and chopped
- 12 large, free-range eggs
- Freshly ground black pepper
- ½ cup crumbled feta

DIRECTIONS:

1. Set the oven to preheat at 350°F. Make sure that the baking rack is placed in the middle of the oven.

2. Place the potatoes in a pot with salted water over medium heat. Once the water is boiling, cook the potatoes for 5-7 minutes, or until softened. Pour the potatoes through a colander over the sink and leave to drain while you prepare the rest of the dish.

3. Heat a large oven-safe pan over medium heat before adding the oil. Add the Swiss chard and fry for about 3 minutes, or until the chard just begins to reduce but is still crisp. Stir in the bell pepper and fry for an additional 5 minutes, or until the peppers are fork-tender but still crisp around the edges. Stir in the potatoes.

4. In a large bowl, whisk the eggs with a pinch of salt and pepper until light and fluffy. Pour the eggs into the pan with your vegetables and gently stir until everything is properly combined.

5. Transfer the pan to a wooden chopping board and sprinkle with the feta in an even layer.

6. Cook the omelet in the middle of the oven for about 20 minutes, or until the eggs are properly cooked and the top is nicely browned. Serve straight away, or keep refrigerated for up to 1 week.

(Tip: You can add all kinds of vegetables to make this omelet more filling, just be sure to check that any additional vegetables rank low on the FODMAP scale.)

BANANA FRENCH TOAST

COOK TIME: 20 MINS | MAKES: 4 SERVINGS

INGREDIENTS:

- 1 tsp. pure vanilla extract
- ¼ tsp. ground nutmeg
- 2 tsp. ground cinnamon
- 3 tbsp. light brown sugar
- 3 large, free-range eggs
- 1 cup almond milk
- 4 tbsp. butter
- 8 slices gluten-free bread
- 1 large, unripe banana (sliced)
- 4 tbsp. pure maple syrup

DIRECTIONS:

1. Whisk together the vanilla, nutmeg, cinnamon, light brown sugar, eggs, and almond milk in a large bowl.

2. Heat a large skillet over medium heat before adding the butter.

3. Once the butter has melted, submerge the bread into the egg mixture for a few seconds until the bread is completely covered. (NOTE: If you leave the bread in the egg mixture for too long, it will become too soggy!)

4. Fry the bread for about 2 minutes per side, or until both sides are golden brown and crispy. Cover the French toast with tin foil, or place in a moderately heated oven while you repeat the frying process with the remaining slices. Add more butter to the skillet as needed.

5. Serve hot with sliced banana and drizzle with pure maple syrup.

(Tip: Bread that is too fresh will make your toast come out soggy, so rather use bread that has been standing for a day or two. Substitute the butter with a dairy-free option if needed.)

HEARTY TURMERIC BEEF TOAST

COOK TIME: 20 MINS | MAKES: 4 SERVINGS

INGREDIENTS:

- 2 tbsp. garlic-infused oil
- 1 lb. ground beef
- 2 tbsp. tomato paste
- 1 tbsp. soy sauce
- 3 tsp. ground turmeric powder
- $1/3$ tsp. cayenne pepper
- Freshly ground black pepper
- Himalayan salt
- ¼ cup spring onions, chopped and whites discarded
- 2 large carrots, peeled and shredded
- 4 cups Swiss chard
- 1 cup chicken broth
- 1 tsp. corn flour
- 8 slices gluten-free bread
- Iceberg lettuce for serving

DIRECTIONS:

1. Heat a large skillet over medium heat before adding the oil and beef. Stir until the beef is nicely browned and cooked through.

2. Stir in the tomato paste, soy sauce, turmeric, and cayenne pepper.

3. Season to taste with salt and pepper before reducing the heat and stirring in the spring onions, carrots, Swiss chard, and chicken broth. Once the mixture is simmering, dissolve the corn flour in 2 tbsp. cold water before stirring it into the skillet.

4. Continue stirring for a few minutes until the sauce has thickened, then remove the skillet from the heat.

5. Toast the bread and top with lettuce. Spoon the mince onto the lettuce and serve.

(Tip: The beef can be frozen or kept in the refrigerator for up to 3 days.)

HEAT-UP BREAKFAST WRAPS

COOK TIME: 20 MINS | MAKES: 8 SERVINGS

INGREDIENTS:

- 3 tbsp. olive oil
- 4 Yukon potatoes, peeled and grated
- ½ red bell pepper, seeded and chopped
- 8 large, free-range eggs
- ½ tsp. paprika
- Kosher salt
- Freshly ground black pepper
- 8 ready-made corn wraps
- 2 cups cheddar, grated

DIRECTIONS:

1. Heat a large pan over medium-high heat before adding 1 tbsp. of the oil. When the oil is hot, sprinkle the grated potatoes into the pan in a single layer. Use a spatula to press the potatoes into the bottom of the pan. Fry for 5-7 minutes, then flip the potatoes and drizzle with 1 tbsp. of olive oil. Fry until the potatoes are nice and crispy. Set aside on a plate and keep warm.

2. Use a wad of greaseproof paper to clean out the pan.

3. Return the pan to the heat and add the last tbsp. of oil. Stir in the bell pepper and fry for 2 minutes until the pepper is tender but the edges are still crisp.

4. In a large bowl, whisk together the eggs and paprika until light and fluffy. Season to taste with salt and pepper. Whisk the egg mixture into the pan with the peppers and stir until the eggs are properly cooked. Remove the pan from the heat.

5. Line the corn wraps up on a clean counter. Divide the fried potatoes between the wraps, and top each wrap with cheese. Spoon the eggs onto the cheese in even amounts. Fold the wraps by tucking the corners in like a burrito.

(Tip: The wraps can be eaten immediately, or wrapped in tin foil and frozen in Ziploc bags for up to 1 month. To heat the wraps, remove the foil and cover with a damp kitchen towel before placing in the microwave for 1-2 minutes – turn the wraps halfway through the heating process.)

SPICY POACHED ITALIAN-STYLE EGGS

COOK TIME: 20 MINS | MAKES: 4 SERVINGS

INGREDIENTS:

- 1 tbsp. garlic-infused oil
- 1 red bell pepper, seeded and chopped
- 1 cup chicken broth
- 1 can crushed tomatoes
- ¼ cup spring onions, chopped and whites discarded
- 2 cups Swiss chard, chopped
- 1 tbsp. corn flour
- Himalayan salt
- Freshly ground black pepper
- ½ tsp. light brown sugar

- ⅛ tsp. cayenne pepper
- 1 tsp. ground cumin
- 1 tsp. paprika
- 4 large, free-range eggs
- 8 slices gluten-free bread
- 2 tbsp. chopped parsley

DIRECTIONS:

1. Place a large skillet over medium-high heat. When the skillet is hot, add in the oil and chopped bell pepper. Fry the pepper until tender but still crispy around the edges.

2. Stir in the chicken broth and crushed tomatoes. Allow the sauce to simmer for 2 minutes.

3. Add the spring onions and Swiss chard.

4. In a small bowl, use a fork to whisk the corn flour into a paste with 2 tbsp. cold water. Add the corn flour paste into the skillet and stir until the sauce thickens.

5. Season to taste with salt and pepper before stirring in the sugar, cayenne pepper, cumin, and paprika. Reduce the heat to medium-low.

6. Make 4 small pockets in the sauce and carefully crack each egg into its own pocket. Place a lid on the skillet and allow the eggs to simmer in the sauce for 10-15 minutes, or until they reach the desired level of doneness.

7. Spoon the eggs along with some of the sauce onto the bread and garnish with parsley before serving.

LUNCH

THAI-GARDEN RICE TOSS

COOK TIME: 30 MINS | MAKES: 4 SERVINGS

INGREDIENTS:

SALAD:
- 2 tbsp. sunflower seeds
- 2 tbsp. pumpkin seeds
- 1 ½ cups frozen edamame, shelled
- ¼ cup spring onions, green leaves chopped and whites discarded
- ½ cup fresh parsley, chopped
- 1 large carrot, peeled and shredded
- 1 cup iceberg lettuce, finely chopped
- 1 ½ cups red cabbage, shredded
- 1 ¼ cups cooked long-grain brown rice

SAUCE:
- ¼ cup sunflower seed butter
- 2 tbsp. soy sauce
- ¼ tsp. cayenne pepper
- 1 tbsp. lemon juice
- ½ tsp. ground ginger
- 1 tsp. sesame seeds
- 1 tbsp. rice wine vinegar
- 1 tbsp. pure maple syrup
- Himalayan salt
- Freshly ground black pepper

DIRECTIONS:

1. In a skillet over medium heat, toast the sunflower and pumpkin seeds until flagrantly roasted. Set aside for garnish.

2. Bring a small pot of water to a boil. Add the frozen edamame and cook for 2 -3 minutes. Drain.

3. In a large bowl, toss together the edamame, spring onion green leaves, parsley, carrots, iceberg lettuce, cabbage, and cooked rice. Set aside while you make the sauce.

4. Place the sunflower seed butter in the microwave for 20 seconds before whisking in the soy sauce, cayenne pepper, lemon juice, ground ginger, sesame seeds, rice wine vinegar, and pure maple syrup. Season to taste with salt and pepper.

5. Drizzle the sauce over the rice and vegetables, toss to coat. Garnish with the toasted seeds and serve.

(Tip: For the sauce, you can substitute the sunflower seed butter with real peanut butter if desired.)

HOMEMADE BURRITO 2-WAYS

COOK TIME: 10 MINS| MAKES: 1 SERVING

INGREDIENTS:

- 2 large, free-range eggs
- ½ tbsp. gluten-free, all-purpose flour
- 1 ½ tbsp. rice milk
- Kosher salt
- Freshly ground black pepper
- Sunflower oil for frying

HAM AND MUSTARD FILLING:
- 1 tsp. French mustard
- Handful Swiss chard, chopped
- 1 ½ oz. sliced ham

VEGGIE FILLING:
- Olive oil for frying
- ½ cup zucchini, chopped
- 1 medium carrot, peeled and julienned
- ½ red bell pepper, sliced into strips
- ½ cup aubergine, sliced
- Himalayan salt
- Freshly ground black pepper
- ¼ tsp. paprika
- Zesty lemon aioli to serve

DIRECTIONS:

1. In a large bowl, whisk together the eggs; gluten-free, all-purpose flour; and rice milk. Season to taste with salt and pepper when the batter is properly combined.

2. Heat a medium-sized skillet over medium-low heat before adding just enough sunflower oil to coat the bottom. When the oil is hot, pour in the batter and gently move the pan from side to side until the batter has evenly coated the bottom.

3. Fry the burrito for 1 minute or until the edges can easily be lifted with a spatula, then flip the burrito and fry the other side for an additional minute, or until the burrito is evenly toasted on either side. Transfer to a plate and keep warm.

4. If using the ham and mustard filling, spread the mustard over the burrito and layer the Swiss chard and ham on top. Fold and serve.

5. If using the veggie filling, fry the vegetables in 1 or 2 tbsp. olive oil. Season to taste with salt and pepper before stirring in the paprika. Place the vegetables in the center of the burrito and drizzle with the zesty lemon aioli. Fold and serve.

(Tips: Although this recipe has two amazing filling options for you to try, the homemade burrito is great with any filling of your choice. These burritos are a fantastic wheat-free alternative for your low-FODMAP diet.)

MAPLE & LIME GLAZED SALMON

COOK TIME: 10 MINS | MAKES: 4 SERVINGS

INGREDIENTS:

- 1 tbsp. apple cider vinegar
- 2 tbsp. pure maple syrup
- 1 lime, juiced
- 1 tbsp. olive oil
- 4 salmon fillets, 6 oz. each

DIRECTIONS:

1. Set the oven to preheat on broil and place a wire rack in the center of the oven.

2. In a large bowl, whisk together the apple cider vinegar, pure maple syrup, lime juice, and olive oil.

3. Place the salmon fillets in the bowl and toss to coat.

4. Cover the bowl and chill for 10 minutes, turning the fillets halfway through. Once the fillets are chilled, transfer the fillets to a plate and place the bowl with the sauce in the microwave for 1 minute on high.

5. Heat a large oven-safe cast-iron pan over medium-high heat. Fry the salmon for 3 minutes before flipping. Use a basting brush to coat the salmon in the heated sauce while the other side cooks for an additional 3 minutes.

6. Remove the pan from the heat and flip each fillet once again before basting them with the sauce.

7. Place the pan in the oven under the broiler for an additional 3 minutes. This will yield medium-rare fillets. You can leave the pan in the oven for a few extra minutes if you prefer them well-done.

8. Plate the salmon fillets and season with salt and pepper to taste before serving.

(Tips: Although apples are a high-FODMAP fruit, apple cider vinegar is low-FODMAP in 2 tbsp. or less. You can substitute the apple cider vinegar with orange or lemon juice if desired.)

MAKI ROLL SHRIMP SALAD

COOK TIME: 15-20 MINS | MAKES: 2-4 SERVINGS

INGREDIENTS:

SAUCE:
- 1 tsp. brown sugar
- 2 tbsp. soy sauce
- 3 tbsp. rice vinegar

SALAD:
- 1 cup uncooked sushi rice
- 2 cups warm water
- 2 tsp. kosher salt
- 12 large shrimp, shelled and deveined

- ½ cup red cabbage, shredded
- 1 medium carrot, peeled and julienned
- 1 large cucumber, peeled and sliced
- ¼ lb. green beans, steamed and drained
- ¼ Hass avocado, peeled and sliced
- 1 sheet toasted nori seaweed, cut into small pieces
- 4 spring onions, thinly sliced
- Wasabi (1 tsp. per serving)
- Low- FODMAP pickled ginger

DIRECTIONS:

1. In a small bowl, whisk together the brown sugar, soy sauce, and rice vinegar. Set aside.

2. In a large pot over medium-high heat, combine the sushi rice, water, and salt. Once the water is boiling, reduce the heat and allow the rice to simmer with the lid on for 12-14 minutes, or until the water has been absorbed. Remove the pot from the heat and allow the rice to stand for 5 minutes before using a fork to separate the grains. Mix in half the marinade and set aside.

3. Fill a medium pot with water and bring to a rolling bowl. Place the shrimp in the water and allow them to cook until they blush (i.e., turn a light shade of pink) and the tails curl into a C. Remove the shrimp from the water immediately and allow them to dry on a paper towel-lined plate.

4. Place the rice in a large serving bowl and top with the shrimp. Arrange the vegetables (cabbage, carrot, cucumber, green beans) over the shrimp, followed by the avocado. Garnish with the nori and spring onions. Serve the dish with the wasabi, pickled ginger, and extra sauce on the side.

(Tip: Limit the avocado to ⅛ per serving, as it is only low-FODMAP in small servings. The shrimp can be substituted with tuna or salmon if desired.)

BUTTERNUT SALAD WITH POMEGRANATE SEEDS

COOK TIME: 20 MINS | MAKES: 3 SERVINGS

INGREDIENTS:

- 2-3 lb. butternut, peeled and cut into small cubes
- Himalayan salt
- Freshly ground black pepper
- ¾ cups olive oil
- ½ cup feta, crumbled
- ½ cup loose pomegranate seeds
- 3 handfuls arugula
- 2 tbsp. lemon juice
- 3-4 oz. grilled chicken breasts (optional)

DIRECTIONS:

1. Set the oven to preheat at 420°F and place the wire rack in the center of the oven.

2. In a large bowl, season the butternut cubes with salt and pepper to taste. Add the oil and toss to coat.

3. Spread the butternut cubes out on a rimmed baking pan. Place the pan in the oven and bake for 20 minutes, tossing the cubes halfway through. The butternut should be fork-tender and slightly crisped around the edges. Set the pan aside on the counter.

4. In a separate bowl, toss together the feta, pomegranate seeds, arugula, and lemon juice. Season to taste with salt and pepper. Add the butternut and toss.

5. If including the chicken: Cut the chicken breasts into strips and add to the salad.

6. If not including the chicken: Serve straightaway.

(Tip: The feta can be substituted with toasted almonds and pumpkin seeds for a dairy-free option.)

HEARTY BEEF & MUSTARD SALAD

COOK TIME: 15 MINS | MAKES: 4 SERVINGS

INGREDIENTS:

- 1 red bell pepper, halved and seeded
- 1 tbsp. olive oil
- Himalayan salt
- Freshly ground black pepper
- 1 ¼ lb. beef sirloin steaks
- 1 ½ cups green beans
- ¼ cup spring onions, chopped and white parts discarded
- 16 baby tomatoes, halved
- 6 cups iceberg lettuce, shredded
- ¼ tsp. brown sugar
- ¼ tsp. black pepper

- ¼ cup olive oil
- 2 tbsp. white vinegar
- 1 ½ tbsp. French mustard

DIRECTIONS:

1. Place the bell pepper open side-down on a baking sheet and scorch in the oven under the grill until the skin turns black. Allow the pepper to cool on the counter before using a knife to remove and discard the blackened skin. Slice the bell pepper into strips and set aside.

2. Use the oil to massage a generous amount of salt and pepper into the sirloin steaks.

3. Heat a large skillet over medium-high heat. Add the steaks to the pan and fry each side until the steaks reach the desired level of doneness (approx. 4 minutes per side for medium-rare). Let the steaks rest for about 5 minutes before slicing into strips.

4. Blanch the green beans in hot water for 5 minutes until they brighten in color. Drain twice using cool water.

5. In a large bowl, toss together the red bell pepper, green beans, spring onions, baby tomatoes, and iceberg lettuce. Arrange the steak strips on top and set aside.

6. In a small bowl, whisk together the sugar, pepper, oil, vinegar, and French mustard. Taste to see if the sauce is right. You can adjust the sourness with a few more pinches of sugar to taste.

7. Drizzle the sauce over the salad and serve.

BOK CHOY TUNA SALAD

COOK TIME: 0 MINS | MAKES: 2-4 SERVINGS

INGREDIENTS:

- 5 oz. canned tuna
- ½ tsp. crushed tarragon
- 1 ½ tsp. fresh lemon juice
- ²/₃ cups low fodmap mayonnaise
- 1 tsp. Dijon mustard
- ¾ cups bok choy stems, chopped
- Flaky sea salt
- Freshly ground black pepper

DIRECTIONS:

1. Use a fine-mesh sieve over the sink to strain as much of the water from the tuna as possible. Use a wooden spoon to press the water out of the tuna. Scrape the drained tuna into a large bowl.

2. Add the crushed tarragon, lemon juice, mayonnaise, mustard, and bok choy stems and mix well. Season to taste with flaky sea salt and black pepper.

3. The tuna salad can be eaten as is, in sandwiches, or as a side.

(Tip: The salad can be refrigerated for up to 3 days in an airtight container. Bok choy is a great celery substitute, as celery is high-FODMAP and needs to be limited to 2" stalk per serving when used.)

BROWN RICE & VEGETABLE BOWL

COOK TIME: 30 MINS | MAKES: 4 SERVINGS

INGREDIENTS:

- 3 cups low-FODMAP vegetables, roasted
- ½ cup spring onions, chopped and white parts discarded
- 3 tbsp. parsley, finely chopped
- 2 cups arugula, chopped
- 2 cups cooked brown rice
- 3 tbsp. roasted pumpkin seeds
- 3 tbsp. feta, crumbled
- Kosher salt
- Freshly ground black pepper
- ½ tsp. brown sugar
- 3 tbsp. olive oil
- 1 ½ tbsp. lemon juice
- 1 ½ tbsp. balsamic vinegar

DIRECTIONS:

1. Roast an assortment of low-FODMAP vegetables in the oven until fork-tender and crisp around the edges. Allow to cool.

2. In a large bowl, toss together the cooled roast vegetables, spring onions, parsley, arugula, cooked rice, pumpkin seeds, and feta. Season to taste with salt and pepper. Set aside while you make the dressing.

3. In a small bowl, whisk together the sugar, olive oil, lemon juice, and balsamic vinegar.

4. Drizzle the dressing over the salad and serve.

FRENCH SALAD WITH MUSTARD DRESSING

COOK TIME: 15 MINS | MAKES: 5 SERVINGS

INGREDIENTS:

- 4 russet potatoes, peeled and cut into wedges
- Kosher salt
- 10 oz. green beans
- 1 tbsp. pure maple syrup
- 4 tbsp. olive oil
- 1 tbsp. French mustard
- 1 tbsp. lemon juice
- 5 oz. tuna, drained
- ¼ cup brown olives, pitted
- 2 tomatoes, diced
- 8 oz. Swiss chard, chopped
- 2 hard-boiled eggs, chopped

DIRECTIONS:

1. Place the potato wedges in a pot of salted water and boil for 10 minutes, or until the wedges are fork-tender, then drain.

2. Blanche the green beans for 5 minutes in boiling water until they brighten. Drain twice using cool water. Allow the potatoes and green beans to drain in a colander over the sink.

3. Meanwhile, in a small bowl, whisk together the pure maple syrup, olive oil, French mustard, and lemon juice until properly combined.

4. In a large bowl, toss the potatoes with 1 tbsp. sauce.

5. Arrange the potatoes, green beans, tuna, olives, tomatoes, Swiss chard, and chopped eggs on a serving platter. Pour the remaining sauce over the entire platter and serve.

(Tip: Olives are low-FODMAP in ½ cup servings and green beans are low-FODMAP in $1/3$ cup servings.)

BEEF & ZUCCHINI STIR-FRY

COOK TIME: 15 MINS | MAKES: 4 SERVINGS

INGREDIENTS:

- 1 tsp. toasted sesame oil
- 1 tsp. fresh ginger, grated
- 1 tbsp. dark brown sugar
- 1 tbsp. oyster sauce
- 3 tbsp. soy sauce
- 8 oz. cooked low-FODMAP Asian rice noodles
- 2 tbsp. garlic-infused olive oil
- 1 lb. beef sirloin fillets, sliced across the grain
- 2 medium carrots, peeled and diced
- 1 cup zucchini, chopped

DIRECTIONS:

1. In a small bowl, whisk together the toasted sesame oil, ginger, dark brown sugar, oyster sauce, and soy sauce. Cover the sauce while you prepare the rest of the dish.

2. In a large bowl, toss the cooked noodles with 1 tbsp. garlic-infused oil and set aside.

3. In a large wok over medium-high heat, heat the remaining olive oil and add in the beef strips. Stir for 4-5 minutes, or until the strips are properly cooked. Scrape the beef into a bowl and keep warm.

4. Return the wok to the stove and fry the carrots and zucchini for 3-4 minutes, or until fork-tender. Toss in the beef and cooked noodles before stirring in the sauce – tossing for 2-3 minutes until everything is evenly coated.

5. Serve immediately.

(Tip: Oyster sauce is low-FODMAP in 1 tbsp. servings.)

HEARTY VEGETARIAN LETTUCE BOWLS

COOK TIME: 0 MINS | MAKES: 1 SERVING

INGREDIENTS:

- ½ cup brown rice
- ½ cup chopped walnuts
- 2 tsp. garlic-infused olive oil
- 3 pickled Jalapeños (whole)
- Himalayan salt
- Freshly ground black pepper
- Iceberg lettuce for serving (center leaves only)

DIRECTIONS:

1. Rinse rice under running water before adding to the pot.

2. Bring a medium pot to boil, using 3 cups of water. Add the rice when boiling and reduce the heat, but keep a steady boil. Cook, uncovered, for 30 minutes. Taste rice to test doneness then drain.

3. Place the walnuts, rice, garlic-infused oil, and jalapenos into a blender and process until you have a lumpy paste. Season to taste with salt and pepper.

4. Spoon the mixture into the lettuce bowl and serve.

NUTTY SUMMER FRUIT SALAD

COOK TIME: 0 MINS | MAKES 4-6 SERVINGS

INGREDIENTS:

- 5 tbsp. brown sugar
- ¼ cup red wine vinegar
- ½ tsp. mustard powder
- ½ tsp. Himalayan salt
- 1 tbsp. poppy seeds
- ½ cup sunflower oil
- 2 tsp. vegan mayonnaise
- 5-6 cups iceberg lettuce, chopped
- ¾ cups toasted pecans, chopped
- ¼ cup cardinal grapes, chopped
- 1 cup pineapple chunks
- ¼ cup fresh blueberries
- ½ cup fresh strawberries, sliced

DIRECTIONS:

1. In a food processor, pulse the sugar and red wine vinegar until most of the sugar granules have dissolved. Mix in the mustard powder, salt, and poppy seeds.

2. With the food processor running on low, gradually pour in the oil and then blend in the mayonnaise. Scrape the sauce into a bowl and chill while you make the salad.

3. In a large bowl, toss the fruit (grapes, pineapple, blueberries, and strawberries), lettuce, and nuts together, along with 4-6 tbsp. dressing. The rest of the dressing can be stored in the fridge for up to 1 week using an airtight container.

(Tip: Cardinal grapes rank very low on the FODMAP scale, so you can indulge as much as you like.)

NUTTY GLUTEN-FREE PASTA SALAD

COOK TIME: 20 MINS | MAKES: 4 SERVINGS

INGREDIENTS:

- 1 lb. gluten-free pasta, cooked al dente
- 2 tbsp. sunflower oil
- 1 cup fresh basil, chopped
- 5 oz. arugula, chopped
- ½ cup toasted almond slivers
- 1 cup feta cheese, crumbled
- Flaky sea salt
- Freshly ground black pepper

DIRECTIONS:

1. Combine the pasta, sunflower oil, basil, and arugula into a large bowl. Toss until everything is properly combined.

2. Mix in the almonds and feta. Season to taste with salt and pepper.

3. Serve straightaway, as this dish does not keep well.

(Tip: The nuts can be replaced with more vegetables and/or pomegranate seeds for dietary requirements.)

MOROCCAN CHICKEN & ORANGE SAUCE

COOK TIME: 10 MINS | MAKES: 2 SERVINGS

INGREDIENTS:

- 1 ½ tsp. Moroccan spice mix
- ½ tbsp. garlic-infused olive oil
- ½ lb. skinless chicken breast, cubed
- Himalayan salt
- Freshly ground black pepper
- ½ tbsp. red wine vinegar
- ½ tbsp. pure maple syrup
- 1 tbsp. freshly squeezed orange juice
- 2 tbsp. sunflower oil
- 1 red bell pepper, seeded and diced

- 1 small cucumber, sliced
- 2 small oranges, peeled and separated
- 2 cups assorted lettuce leaves, torn

DIRECTIONS:

1. In a large bowl, toss together the Moroccan spice, garlic-infused oil, chicken cubes, and a generous pinch of salt and pepper until the chicken is properly coated.

2. Place a non-stick skillet over medium heat. When the skillet is hot, fry the chicken for 3-4 minutes, or until golden brown. Transfer to a bowl. (NOTE: The chicken is even better when cooked the day before and left in the fridge overnight.)

3. In a small glass bowl, whisk together the red wine vinegar, pure maple syrup, orange juice, and sunflower oil. Season to taste with salt and pepper. Set aside.

4. Place the ingredients in jars, starting with the orange sauce, followed by the bell pepper, cucumber, chicken, orange segments, and lettuce leaves. Do not shake the jar until you are ready to eat the salad. Placing the layers in this order will ensure the freshness of ingredients while being stored.

5. Chill and grab on the go.

CARAMELIZED AUTUMN SALAD

COOK TIME: 35 MINS | MAKES: 4 SERVINGS

INGREDIENTS:

- 10 ½ oz. pumpkin, peeled and seeded
- Himalayan salt
- Freshly ground black pepper
- Garlic-infused olive oil
- 8 oz. canned whole beets, drained and patted dry
- ½ tsp. paprika
- ¼ cup mixed sunflower and sesame seeds
- 1 tbsp. butter
- ⅛ tsp. ground cinnamon
- 2 tsp. orange peel, grated
- 1 large orange, juiced
- 2 tbsp. dark brown sugar

- ½ cup fresh mint leaves, chopped
- 3 cups mixed lettuce, chopped
- 2-3 tbsp. feta cheese, crumbled

DIRECTIONS:

1. Set the oven to preheat at 400°F. Place a wire rack in the center of the oven.
2. Chop the pumpkin into ¾" cubes and place them in a large bowl. Sprinkle the cubes generously with salt and pepper before adding about 2 tbsp. oil. Toss until the cubes are evenly coated.
3. Arrange the seasoned cubes on a baking sheet, along with the beets, and bake in the oven until the pumpkin is golden brown and fork-tender (approx. 20-25 minutes – flip the vegetables halfway through the cooking time).
4. Heat a large skillet over medium heat. When the skillet is hot, add 1 tsp oil, then toss in the mixed seeds, paprika and roast until the seeds are toasted. Scrape into a bowl and leave to cool.
5. Remove the pan from the oven and allow the vegetables to cool before quartering the beets.
6. Return the skillet to the heat. When the skillet is hot, melt the butter. Add the cinnamon, orange peel, orange juice, and sugar to the skillet, stirring continuously.
7. Add the pumpkin and beets to the skillet when the sauce begins to thicken. Stir until most of the liquid has been absorbed and the vegetables are nicely glazed (approx. 2-3 minutes).
8. Scrape the caramelized vegetables into a large serving bowl and toss with the mint leaves and lettuce until everything is properly combined. Garnish with feta and toasted seeds before serving.

NUTTY CHICKEN & MUSTARD SALAD

COOK TIME: 0 MINS | MAKES: 3-4 SERVINGS

INGREDIENTS:

- 2 tsp. lemon juice
- 1 tbsp. French mustard
- 2 tbsp. crushed tarragon
- ¼ cup tangy mayonnaise
- 2 cups cooked chicken, diced
- Flaky sea salt
- Freshly ground black pepper
- 2 tbsp. lightly toasted pecans, chopped
- ½ cup seedless cardinal grapes

DIRECTIONS:

1. Combine the lemon juice, mustard, tarragon, mayonnaise, and chicken into a large bowl. Stir gently until everything is properly combined. Season to taste with salt and pepper.

2. Gently stir in the pecans and grapes. Serve as is, or as a sandwich filling on gluten-free bread.

(Tip: Be mindful when using store-bought cooked chicken as they may not have used FODMAP-friendly ingredients in the cooking process.)

BLUE CHEESE BACON SALAD

COOK TIME: 15-20 MINS | MAKES: 2-4 SERVINGS

INGREDIENTS:

- 2 tbsp. spring onions, chopped (green parts only)
- 2 oz. blue cheese, crumbled
- ½ cup seedless cardinal grapes, halved
- 4 oz. baby spinach, chopped
- 2 slices thick-cut bacon, cubed
- 1 tsp. brown sugar
- 1 tsp. French mustard
- 2 tbsp. red wine vinegar
- Himalayan salt
- Freshly ground black pepper
- Olive oil (optional)

DIRECTIONS:

1. In a large bowl, toss together the spring onions, blue cheese, grapes, and baby spinach. Set aside while you prepare the rest of the dish.

2. In a medium pan, fry the bacon until the edges are nice and crisp, Transfer the crispy bacon to a paper towel-lined plate. With the bacon fat still in the pan, stir in the sugar, mustard, and red wine vinegar until everything is properly combined. Season to taste with salt and pepper, then add in the olive oil. (NOTE: You can simply omit the olive oil if you like.)

3. Pour the hot sauce into the bowl with the salad and top with the crispy bacon cubes. Toss and serve straight away.

(Tips: Not all blue cheese is gluten-free. Replace the blue cheese with feta to suit your dietary requirements.)

LOW-FODMAP TOASTED TUNA SANDWICH

COOK TIME: 5 MINS | MAKES: 1 SERVING

INGREDIENTS:

- 2 tbsp. spring onions, chopped (green parts only)
- 1 tbsp. parsley, chopped
- ¼ tsp. paprika
- 1 tsp. lemon juice
- 2 tbsp. low fodmap mayonnaise
- 3 oz. canned tuna in spring water, drained
- Flaky sea salt
- Freshly ground black pepper
- 2 slices gluten-free bread
- 2 thin slices mozzarella

DIRECTIONS:

1. Set the broiler in the oven to preheat.

2. In a large bowl, combine the spring onions, parsley, paprika, lemon juice, vegan mayonnaise, and tuna. Mix well and season to taste with salt and pepper.

3. Place the bread on a baking sheet. Divide the tuna between the two slices and spread it out evenly. Arrange the cheese on top of the tuna and broil in the oven until the cheese has melted.

4. Serve straight away.

(Tip: If you prefer much harder toast, toast the bread before topping with the tuna.)

ITALIAN-HERB PASTA SALAD

COOK TIME: 10-15 MINS | MAKES: 6-8 SERVINGS

INGREDIENTS:

- Sea salt
- 12 oz. brown rice spiral pasta
- 2 tsp. French mustard
- 2 tbsp. red wine vinegar
- ¼ cup garlic-infused olive oil
- Freshly ground black pepper
- 2 cups baby tomatoes, halved
- 4 oz. goat cheese, crumbled
- ½ cup fresh basil leaves, torn
- 1 cup arugula

DIRECTIONS:

1. Bring 5 qts of salted water to a rolling boil before adding in the pasta. Cook until al dente. (NOTE: This kind of pasta cooks really quickly, so keep an eye on it while you prepare the rest of the dish.)

2. Meanwhile, in a small bowl, whisk together the mustard, vinegar, and olive oil.

3. Pour the cooked pasta through a colander set over the sink and rinse twice with cool water. Transfer to a large bowl and toss with ¼ of the sauce. Season with salt and pepper.

4. Stir in the tomatoes and cheese. Add more dressing if needed – you don't have to use all of the dressing. Toss in the basil and baby arugula.

5. Serve straight away, as this salad does not keep well.

DINNER

ZESTY ASIAN-STYLE CHICKEN

COOK TIME: 40 MINS | MAKES: 4 SERVINGS

INGREDIENTS:

- 1 tsp. crushed ginger
- 1 tbsp. garlic-infused oil
- 4 tbsp. pure maple syrup
- 4 tbsp. low-sodium soy sauce
- 2 tbsp. lemon juice
- 1 tsp. finely grated lemon peel
- 1 ¼ lbs. boneless chicken thighs
- 2 ½ cups low-FODMAP chicken broth
- 2 cups Japanese pumpkin, peeled and diced

- 2 large carrots, peeled and diced
- 1 ½ cups long-grain brown rice
- 1 cup chopped leeks (green parts only)
- 1 tbsp. garlic-infused oil
- 1 ½ cups green beans, chopped
- 3 tbsp. cilantro, chopped
- Kosher salt
- Freshly ground black pepper

DIRECTIONS:

1. Butter a deep oven dish and set the oven to preheat at 375°F. Place a wire rack in the center of the oven.

2. In a large bowl, whisk together the ginger, garlic-infused oil, pure maple syrup, soy sauce, lemon juice, and finely grated lemon peel. Submerge the chicken thighs in the marinade and let stand for 15-60 minutes.

3. Heat the chicken broth in a pot on the stove, or for 1-2 minutes in the microwave using a micro-wave-safe bowl.

4. Toss the Japanese pumpkin and carrots into a large bowl with 3 tbsp. water, until everything is evenly coated. Place the bowl in the microwave on high until the vegetables are tender. Pour the vegetables through a colander set over the sink and allow to drain.

5. Once the vegetables are mostly dry, place them in a large bowl along with the rice and leeks.

6. Transfer the chicken to a separate bowl and place 3 tbsp. marinade in a small glass bowl. Stir the rest of the marinade into the bowl until everything is evenly coated before pouring the contents of the bowl into the prepared baking dish. Seal the dish with tin foil and bake in the oven for 30-40 minutes, or until the rice is cooked. Stir once, halfway through.

7. Heat a large skillet over medium-high heat before adding the garlic-infused olive oil and frying the chicken breasts for 4 minutes on each side. The chicken will not be properly cooked at this stage.

8. Place the chicken thighs on a baking sheet and use a basting brush to marinate the chicken with half of the reserved marinade. Place the tray in the oven for 10 minutes before basting again. Bake for an additional 5 minutes, or until the thighs are properly cooked.

9. Blanch the green beans a few minutes before serving. Once they are properly drained, stir them into the rice and vegetables along with all the sauce from the chicken and remaining marinade. Arrange the thighs on top of the rice and sprinkle with chopped cilantro before seasoning to taste with salt and pepper.

10. Serve and enjoy!

SPICY HAM AND SHRIMP JAMBALAYA

COOK TIME: 1 HOUR | MAKES: 4 SERVINGS

INGREDIENTS:

- 1 lb. large shrimp, deveined with shells on
- ½ tsp. red pepper flakes
- ½ tsp. crushed thyme
- ½ tsp. crushed oregano
- ½ tsp. freshly ground black pepper
- 1 tsp. Himalayan salt
- 1 tsp. paprika
- 2 tbsp. garlic-infused olive oil
- 1 medium shallot, peeled and halved
- 1 celery stalk, chopped and diced
- 1 green bell pepper, cored, seeded, and sliced
- ½ cup spring onions, chopped (green sections only)
- 5 oz. ham cut into ¼" cubes
- 1 can diced tomatoes
- 1 bay leaf
- 1 cup long-grain brown rice

DIRECTIONS:

1. Remove the shells from the shrimp and set the shrimp aside. Bring the shells to a boil in a large pot with 3 cups of water. Once the water has reached a rolling boil, reduce the heat and allow the water to simmer for 5 minutes.

2. Meanwhile, in a small glass bowl, whisk together the red pepper flakes, thyme, oregano, black pepper, salt, and paprika. Place the peeled shrimp in a large bowl and toss with half of the spice mixture until evenly coated.

3. Strain 2 cups of the shrimp broth and discard the shells along with the remaining stock.

4. Heat a large frying pan over medium-high heat before adding the oil and shallots, face down, in the pan. Fry the shallots for a few minutes before removing them from the pan right before they begin to brown. (Note: Discard the shallots as they are very high-FODMAP – the taste will remain in the oil while still keeping the dish low-FODMAP.)

5. Add the celery and bell pepper. Stir until the vegetables are just fork-tender.

6. Stir in half of the spring onions and all of the ham. Add the remaining spice mixture and toss to coat.

7. Fry the mixture in the spice for 30 seconds. Toss in the two cups of stock, along with the tomatoes and bay leaf. Stir until the sauce just begins to simmer before lowering the heat and mixing in the rice. Allow the rice to simmer for about 25 minutes or until the rice is properly cooked and most of the sauce has been absorbed.

8. Add the shrimp to the rice and simmer for 5 minutes until the shrimp blush and curl into a C shape.

9. Spoon the rice into bowls and garnish with the remaining spring onions before serving.

(Tip: This recipe uses ham in place of sausage, as sausage can be high-FODMAP due to the varying ingredients used in making it.)

CHEESY BAKED BEEF WRAPS

COOK TIME: 15 MINS | MAKES: 4 SERVINGS

INGREDIENTS:

- 1 can plain crushed tomatoes
- ¼ tsp. Kosher salt
- ¼ tsp. freshly ground black pepper
- ¼ tsp. cayenne pepper
- 1 tsp. brown sugar
- 1 ½ tsp. ground cilantro seeds
- 2 tsp. ground cumin
- 2 tsp. crushed oregano
- 4 tsp. paprika
- 2 tbsp. tomato paste
- ½ cup low-FODMAP chicken broth
- 1 tbsp. corn flour

- 8 corn wraps
- 3 tsp. garlic-infused olive oil
- 1 lb. ground beef
- 1 cup leeks, chopped (green leaves only)
- ½ cup mozzarella, grated
- 2 cups shredded purple cabbage
- 1 cup shredded iceberg lettuce
- 2 medium carrots, shredded
- 1 tbsp. fresh lemon juice
- Parsley for garnish

DIRECTIONS:

1. Puree the tomatoes in a food processor before placing them in a pot over medium heat along with the salt, pepper, cayenne pepper, sugar, cilantro seeds, cumin, oregano, paprika, tomato paste, and chicken broth. Bring the mixture to simmer, stirring occasionally.

2. Whisk the corn flour in a small bowl with 2 tbsp. cold water to form a paste. Whisk the corn flour paste into the simmering sauce and stir for 1-2 minutes until the sauce begins to thicken. Set aside off the heat.

3. Heat the wraps in the microwave or a moderate oven. (Note: Cold wraps will likely break if you bake them straight away at high temperatures.)

4. Heat a large skillet over medium-high heat before adding the oil and browning the beef. When the beef is nicely browned, stir in the leeks. Scoop ¾ cups of the sauce into a small bowl and set aside before stirring the remaining sauce into the beef and simmering for 2 minutes.

5. Butter a large casserole dish and set the oven to preheat at 350°F. Place a wire rack in the center of the oven.

6. Place the wraps opened in the casserole dish and spoon in equal amounts of mince and sauce onto each wrap. Fold the warps like burritos and pour the remaining sauce over the folded wraps. Sprinkle the grated cheese over the wraps and sauce. Place the dish in the oven for 15 minutes until the cheese is bubbling.

7. While the wraps are baking, combine the cabbage, lettuce, carrots, and lemon juice in a large bowl. Season to taste with salt and pepper if needed.

8. Plate the wraps, sprinkle with parsley, and serve with a side of coleslaw.

(Tip: Mozzarella is low-FODMAP at 1 ½ ounces per serving.)

WILD RICE & GINGER COD

COOK TIME: 10 MINS | MAKES: 2 SERVINGS

INGREDIENTS:

- 2 skinless cod fillets
- Flaky sea salt
- Freshly ground black pepper
- 2 tbsp. fresh ginger, peeled and grated
- 2 tbsp. low-sodium soy sauce
- 3 tbsp. clear apple cider vinegar
- 6 spring onions cut into strips
- 2 cups wild rice (cooked for serving)

DIRECTIONS:

1. Massage the cod fillets with a generous amount of salt and pepper and set aside.
2. In a small saucepan over medium-high heat, whisk together the ginger, soy sauce, and apple cider vinegar.
3. Once the sauce is simmering, place the cod fillets in the sauce and bring to a boil. Place the lid on the pot and simmer for 6-8 minutes until the fish is opaque and can easily break apart with a fork. Arrange the spring onions over the fish and boil for an additional 3 minutes.
4. Serve the fish immediately on a bed of wild rice with the sauce spooned over everything.

LOW-FODMAP CHICKEN CURRY

COOK TIME: 20 MINS | MAKES: 2 SERVINGS

INGREDIENTS:

- 1 tbsp. coconut oil
- 1 red bell pepper, diced
- 1 spring onion, chopped
- 3 large skinless chicken breasts, sliced into small cubes
- 2 tbsp. turmeric powder
- 1 tbsp. curry powder
- 2 tins unsweetened coconut milk
- Himalayan salt
- Freshly ground black pepper
- 2 cups basmati rice, cooked for serving

DIRECTIONS:

1. Melt the coconut oil in a large frying pan over medium-high heat before stirring in the bell pepper and spring onion. Fry the vegetables for 3-5 minutes, or until fork-tender.
2. Stir in the chicken cubes and fry for about 7 minutes, or until properly cooked.
3. Whisk in the turmeric, curry powder, and unsweetened coconut milk. Season to taste with salt and pepper.
4. Serve the hot curry on a bed of cooked basmati rice. You can refrigerate the dish for up to 1 week in a sealed container.

ITALIAN-STYLE PASTA & SHRIMP

COOK TIME: 20 MINS | MAKES: 6 SERVINGS

INGREDIENTS:

- 8 oz. gluten-free pasta
- 2 tbsp. garlic-infused olive oil
- 6 tbsp. butter
- 1 tsp. cayenne pepper
- 11 lb. large shrimp, deveined and shelled
- 4 cups baby spinach
- ½ tsp. crushed oregano
- ½ tsp. crushed thyme
- ½ tsp. crushed basil
- 2 tbsp. parsley, chopped
- ½ cup parmesan cheese, shredded
- 1 tbsp. lemon juice

DIRECTIONS:

1. Fill a large pot with salted water and bring to a rolling boil over medium-high heat. Once the water is boiling, add the pasta and cook to the desired level of doneness. Pour the cooked pasta through a colander over the sink and allow to drain before transferring to a bowl and tossing with 1 tbsp. oil.

2. In a large pot over medium-high heat, melt 2 tbsp. butter with 1 tbsp. oil. When the butter is bubbling, whisk in the cayenne pepper and add the shrimp. Fry the shrimp for 5 minutes, or until they blush and the tails curl into a C shape. Stir in the baby spinach, oregano, thyme, and basil; cooking the spinach until it has reduced to about half its size.

3. Add the cooked pasta, parsley, remaining butter, and parmesan to the pot. Stir until everything is properly combined.

4. Plate the pasta and drizzle with the lemon juice before serving.

(Tip: Baby spinach is low-FODMAP in servings as big as 11 ½ cups.)

CHEESY SPINACH-STUFFED FILET MIGNON

COOK TIME: 40 MINS | MAKES: 8-10 SERVINGS

INGREDIENTS:

- 1 tbsp. + 1 tsp. garlic-infused olive oil
- 2 large tomatoes, seeded and chopped
- 1 tsp. tomato purée
- Himalayan salt
- Freshly ground black pepper
- 8 oz. chevre, grated
- 10 oz. Swiss chard

- 1 filet mignon (4-5 lbs.)
- ½ tsp. crushed rosemary
- ½ tsp. crushed thyme
- ½ tsp. lavender
- ½ tsp. tarragon

DIRECTIONS:

1. Set the oven to preheat at 450°F with the wire rack in the middle of the oven.

2. In a medium pot over medium-high heat, heat 1 tsp. olive oil and add the tomatoes and tomato purée. Cook the ingredients for about 15 minutes, or until the liquid has reduced and the tomatoes have made a thick paste. Set aside off the heat.

3. Once the tomato paste has cooled, stir in the cheese and Swiss chard until properly mixed.

4. Place the filet on a wooden chopping board and slice a pocket along the length of the meat (Note: Be careful not to slice all the way through!). Massage the filet all over with a generous amount of salt and pepper along with the rosemary, thyme, lavender, and tarragon.

5. Spoon the tomato mixture into the pocket, packing it in as tightly as possible. Use butcher's twine to secure the filet in 2 or 3 sections. Use a basting brush to coat the filet in the remaining oil.

6. Place the filet in a baking dish and roast in the oven for about 25 minutes for medium-rare, or until cooked to your liking.

7. Remove the dish from the oven and cover with tin foil. Allow the meat to stand on the counter for 5 minutes before slicing and serving.

8. You can serve the meat straight away or cooled – use any accumulated juices from the dish as a sauce for your meat.

(Tips: The meat can be seasoned and chilled for 24 hours before roasting. The meat should be warmed to room temperature before baking if chilled for 24 hours.)

MEXICAN-STYLE FISH WRAPS

COOK TIME: 10 MINS | MAKES: 4 SERVINGS

INGREDIENTS:

- ¼ cup vegan mayonnaise
- 1 cup red cabbage, shredded
- 1 cup green cabbage, shredded
- 1 ½ fresh limes, juiced
- ¼ cup taco seasoning
- 1 lb. halibut fillets
- 1 tbsp. sunflower sauce
- 8 corn wraps

- ½ cup restaurant-style salsa
- ½ avocado, sliced into 8 slices
- Cilantro, chopped for serving
- Lime wedges for serving

DIRECTIONS:

1. Combine the mayonnaise, red cabbage, green cabbage, and half of the lime juice in a large bowl.

2. In a separate large bowl, whisk together the remaining lime juice and taco seasoning. Submerge the fillets in the sauce and chill for 10 minutes, turning the fish after 5 minutes. Transfer the fish to a plate and discard the sauce.

3. Heat a large frying pan over medium-high heat before adding the oil and frying the fish for 3-4 minutes on each side, or until opaque.

4. Heat the wraps in the microwave or a moderate oven. To build the wraps, place the them on the counter and fill with equal amounts of the cooked fish before topping with salsa and avocado slices.

5. Fold the wraps and garnish with the cilantro. Serve with the with lime wedges on the side.

(Tip: Limit the avocado to ⅛th per serving for a low-FODMAP diet.)

AUTUMN PASTA WITH CRISPY BACON

COOK TIME: 30 MINS | MAKES: 4 SERVINGS

INGREDIENTS:

- 2 large carrots, peeled and cubed
- 2 cups Japanese pumpkin, peeled and cubed
- 3 tbsp. garlic-infused olive oil
- ½ lb. bacon, cubed
- 3 tbsp. fresh sage, chopped
- ¾ cups finely chopped leeks (green parts only)
- Sea salt
- Freshly ground black pepper
- 2 cups low-FODMAP chicken broth
- 10 oz. gluten-free pasta
- 4 cups Swiss chard, roughly chopped
- 2 tbsp. parmesan cheese, shredded

DIRECTIONS:

1. Toss the carrots and pumpkin cubes in a large bowl with 2 tbsp. water until evenly coated. Microwave for 2-3 minutes on high.

2. Heat a large skillet over medium-high heat before adding 2 tbsp. oil and fry the bacon until the edges are nice and crispy.

3. Stir in the vegetables, sage, and leaks. Season to taste with salt and pepper. After 5 minutes, stir in the chicken broth. When the broth is boiling, lower the heat and cook for about 10 minutes, or until the carrots are completely soft and the liquid has reduced by half.

4. Fill a large pot with salted water and the remaining oil, and bring to a rolling boil over medium-high heat. Once the water is boiling, add the pasta and cook until al dente. Reserve one cup of the water before draining the pasta in a colander set over the sink.

5. Use a hand-held blender to process the cooked vegetables into a lump-free sauce. Beat ¼ cup of the reserved pasta water into the sauce (or more if needed) until it reaches the desired consistency. Fold the Swiss chard into the cooked pasta.

6. Plate the pasta and serve topped with the crispy bacon and shredded parmesan.

SWEET & SPICY GLAZED CHICKEN

COOK TIME: 25 MINS | MAKES: 6 SERVINGS

INGREDIENTS:

- ¾ tsp. ground cumin
- 1 ½ tsp. ground paprika
- ¾ tsp. ground cinnamon
- 1 whole chicken, cut into pieces
- 1 1/2 tbsp. French mustard
- 2 tbsp. butter
- 3 tbsp. pure maple syrup
- Himalayan salt
- Freshly ground black pepper

DIRECTIONS:

1. Cover a baking tray with tin foil and lightly coat the tin foil with baking spray. Set the oven to preheat at 500°F. Place a wire rack in the center of the oven.

2. In a small glass bowl, whisk together the cumin, paprika, and cinnamon. Place the chicken pieces skin side up on the prepared baking tray and massage the spice mixture into the pieces in an even layer before baking in the oven for about 15 minutes.

3. While the chicken is baking, place the mustard, butter, and pure maple syrup in a glass bowl. Place the bowl in the microwave on high until the butter is bubbling, whisking every 30 seconds.

4. Once the chicken has been in the oven for 15 minutes, use a basting brush to coat the chicken in the marinade. Place the tray back in the oven and bake for an additional 5 minutes. Repeat the process one more time until the chicken is properly cooked.

PAN FRIED TILAPIA WITH OLIVES

COOK TIME: 10 MINS | MAKES: 4 SERVINGS

INGREDIENTS:

- 4 tilapia fillets, patted dry
- Flaky sea salt
- Freshly ground black pepper
- 3 tbsp. avocado oil
- ½ cup parsley, chopped
- ½ cup brown olives, pitted and halved
- 2 cups cherry tomatoes, halved
- 1 tbsp. lemon juice

DIRECTIONS:

1. Season both sides of the tilapia fillets with salt and pepper. Set aside.

2. Heat a large frying pan over medium-high heat before adding the oil and frying the fish for 3 minutes per side until the fish is opaque. Place the cooked fish in a dish and cover with tin foil.

3. Return the pan to the heat and add the parsley, olives, and tomatoes. Fry for 3 minutes before adding the lemon juice and seasoning to taste with a pinch of salt and pepper.

4. Plate the fish and top with the olive sauce before serving.

(Tip: Olives are low-FODMAP in servings of ½ cup.)

ONE-PAN TURKEY & CORN BREAD

COOK TIME: 30 MINS | MAKE: 6 SERVINGS

INGREDIENTS:

TURKEY:
- 1 tbsp. garlic-infused olive oil
- ¼ cup leeks, chopped (green parts only)
- ½ medium-sized green bell pepper, seeded and chopped
- 1 ½ lbs. ground turkey
- ½ tsp. ground oregano
- ½ tsp. ground cumin
- Himalayan salt
- Freshly ground black pepper
- 1 tbsp. tomato puree
- 1 tin fire-roasted diced tomatoes

CORN BREAD:
- 1 tsp. lemon juice
- ½ cup lactose-free milk
- 1 large free-range egg
- 3 tbsp. butter melted
- ¼ tsp. bicarbonate of soda
- ¼ tsp. Kosher salt
- 1 tsp. baking powder
- ⅓ cup gluten-free all-purpose flour
- ⅔ cups stone-ground yellow cornmeal
- ¼ cup spring onions, chopped (green parts only)
- 2 ½ oz. extra-sharp cheddar cheese

DIRECTIONS:

1. Set the oven to preheat at 400°F. Place a wire rack in the center of the oven.

2. Heat a large cast-iron pan over medium-high heat before adding the oil and frying the leeks and bell pepper for about 5 minutes until fork-tender.

3. Stir the turkey into the skillet and fry for an additional 5 minutes, or until the meat is no longer pink. Add the oregano and cumin. Season to taste with salt and pepper.

4. Stir in the tomato puree and diced tomatoes. Allow the sauce to simmer for 5 minutes. Adjust the seasoning after tasting if desired.

5. Meanwhile, in a small bowl, beat the lemon juice and milk. Allow the mixture to rest undisturbed on the counter for 5 minutes. Once the mixture has curdled. Whisk in the egg and melted butter.

6. In a separate bowl, whisk together the bicarbonate of soda, Kosher salt, baking powder, all-purpose flour, and cornmeal.

7. Add the milk and lemon mixture to the dry ingredients and gently fold in the spring onions and cheese until the mixture just comes together. Do not over mix.

8. When the turkey is done and still simmering in the pan, carefully spoon the cornbread mixture onto it. Bake the turkey in the oven for 15-20 minutes, or until an inserted skewer comes out dry. Serve straight away.

CILANTRO PORK & STIR-FRY VEGETABLES

COOK TIME: 20 MINS | MAKES: 4 SERVINGS

INGREDIENTS:

- 1 large free-range egg, lightly beaten
- 1 tbsp. garlic-infused olive oil
- ½ cup gluten-free breadcrumbs
- 2 tbsp. light brown sugar
- ¼ tsp. cayenne pepper
- 2 tbsp. fresh lemongrass, chopped
- 3 ½ tbsp. fresh cilantro, chopped
- 1 lb. ground pork
- Himalayan salt
- Freshly ground black pepper
- Olive oil for frying
- 1 tbsp. toasted sesame oil

- ¼ cup spring onions, chopped
- 2 large carrots, peeled and chopped
- 1 tsp. fresh ginger, grated
- 1 tbsp. water
- 3 tbsp. soy sauce
- 4 cups Bok choy, sliced
- 1 ¼ cup basmati rice, cooked for serving

DIRECTIONS:

1. In a large bowl, use a wooden spoon to combine the egg, garlic-infused oil, breadcrumbs, sugar, cayenne pepper, lemongrass, cilantro, ground pork, and a pinch of salt and pepper to taste. When the ingredients are properly combined, roll the mixture into 24 bite-sized balls and set aside.

2. Heat a large skillet over medium-high heat before adding the garlic-infused oil. When the oil is hot, fry the meatballs in batches until evenly browned and properly cooked. Place the cooked meatballs in a dish and cover with tin foil to keep warm, or place in a moderate oven.

3. Return the skillet to the heat with the toasted sesame oil and fry the spring onions, carrots, and fresh ginger for 2-3 minutes. Add the water, soy sauce, and bok choy to the skillet and toss for an additional 1-2 minutes.

4. Serve the stir-fried vegetables on a bed of cooked rice and top with the meatballs to serve.

QUICK ITALIAN HERB CHICKEN

COOK TIME: 25 MINS | MAKES: 4 SERVINGS

INGREDIENTS:

- 2 tbsp. garlic-infused olive oil
- 4 skinless chicken breasts
- Himalayan salt
- Freshly ground black pepper
- 3 tsp. Italian seasoning
- 1 cup raw quinoa
- 2 cups chicken stock
- 3 tbsp. lemon juice

DIRECTIONS:

1. Heat a large frying pan over medium-high heat before adding 1 tbsp. olive oil. When the oil is hot, add the chicken and season with a pinch of salt and pepper, along with 1 tsp. Italian seasoning. Sear each side for about 2 minutes. The chicken will not be completely cooked at this point. Set aside on a platter while you prepare the rest of the dish.

2. Return the pan to the heat and add the remaining oil along with the quinoa. Toss until the quinoa is properly coated.

3. Stir in the remaining Italian seasoning, chicken stock, and lemon juice before adding the seared chicken. Once the stock is simmering, place the lid on the pot and simmer until all of the liquid has been absorbed and the quinoa is puffy (approx. 20 minutes).

4. Plate and serve hot.

TANGY GROUND TURKEY BUNS

COOK TIME: 15 MINS | MAKES: 6 SERVINGS

INGREDIENTS:

- 1 tbsp. avocado oil
- 1 lb. ground turkey
- ¼ cup light corn syrup
- ¼ cup tomato sauce
- 3 tbsp. soy sauce
- 3 tbsp corn flour
- ½ cup low-FODMAP chicken broth
- Sea salt
- Freshly ground black pepper
- 6 gluten-free hamburger buns

DIRECTIONS:

1. Heat a large skillet over medium-high heat before adding the oil and frying the ground turkey for 3-5 minutes. Use a spatula to hold back the ground turkey as you pour off most of the fat. Place the skillet with the drained meat back on the stove and stir in the corn syrup, tomato sauce, and soy sauce.

2. While the meat and sauce are simmering, whisk together the corn flour and chicken broth in a small bowl. Whisk the broth into the skillet and stir for 5-8 minutes, or until the sauce thickens. Add salt and pepper to taste.

3. Serve the ground turkey and sauce in the hamburger buns.

(Tip: Corn syrup with low fructose levels can be consumed on a low-FODMAP diet. Tomato sauce should be served in servings of 2 tsp. or less with brands that contain low-fructose levels.)

DECADENT LOW-FODMAP LASAGNA

COOK TIME: 1-2 HOURS | MAKES: 8-10 SERVINGS

INGREDIENTS:

- 4 oz. bacon, cubed
- ¼ lb. ground pork
- ¾ lb. ground beef
- 2 tsp. garlic-infused olive oil
- 4 cups tomato puree
- ½ tsp. crushed fennel seeds
- ½ tsp. crushed oregano
- ¼ tsp. cayenne pepper
- Himalayan salt
- Freshly ground black pepper
- 10 oz. gluten-free lasagne sheets
- 2 tbsp. parsley, chopped

- 1 lb. lactose-free cottage cheese (such as Green Valley Creamery Lactose Free Organic Cottage Cheese)
- ½ cup parmesan, grated
- 1 large free-range egg
- 1 lb. mozzarella, grated

DIRECTIONS:

1. Heat a large frying pan over medium-high heat before adding the bacon and frying for about 3 minutes, or until the edges are nice and crispy. Stir in the pork and beef. Fry for an additional 5 minutes, or until all of the meat is properly cooked. Use a slotted spoon to transfer the meat to a paper-lined plate and discard all of the oil in the pot before wiping away any excess oil.

2. Return the pan to the heat and add the garlic-infused olive oil along with the fried meat, tomato puree, fennel seeds, oregano, and cayenne pepper. Add salt and pepper to taste. When the sauce begins to simmer, lower the heat and simmer for 15 minutes with the lid on, stirring occasionally while keeping an eye on the heat.

3. Set the oven to preheat at 350°F with the wire rack in the middle of the oven.

4. In a large bowl, whisk together the parsley, cottage cheese, parmesan, and egg. Add a pinch of salt and pepper and whisk to incorporate.

5. Begin layering the lasagne into a large 13 x 9" casserole dish. Start with a layer of meat and sauce, followed by 3-4 lasagne sheets. The sheets should just be touching but not overlapping. Add a thin layer of the egg and cheese mixture followed by another thin layer of the meat and sauce topped with some of the mozzarella. Repeat the process until you finish with a final layer of mozzarella. Sprinkle the parmesan over the top and bake for 50-60 minutes, or until the cheese is bubbling and the top is golden brown.

6. Remove the casserole dish from the oven and allow the lasagne to rest for 5 minutes before slicing and serving hot.

(Tips: Fennel seeds are low-FODMAP while fennel tea is not. Normal store-bought cottage cheese is not usually low-FODMAP, so be cautious when purchasing your cheese.)

SPICY JAMAICAN SHREDDED PORK

COOK TIME: 10 HOURS | MAKES: 6 SERVINGS

INGREDIENTS:

Pork:
- 3 tbsp. tomato puree
- 2 tbsp. dark brown sugar
- ¼ tsp. cayenne pepper
- 1 tsp. dried chives
- 1 tsp. ground cinnamon
- 1 tsp. allspice
- 2 tsp. crushed thyme
- 3 tsp. paprika
- 1 ¼ lb. skinless pork shoulder roast
- 3 large carrots, peeled and diced
- 1 cup leeks, chopped (green parts only)
- 2 cups low-FODMAP chicken broth
- 2 tsp. ground ginger

- Himalayan salt
- Freshly ground black pepper
- 2 tsp. garlic-infused olive oil

Salsa:
- 3 tbsp. cilantro, chopped
- ¼ cup spring onions, chopped (green parts only)
- 1 can pineapple pieces, drained
- 1 red bell pepper, seeded and diced

Gravy:
- 2 tsp. corn flour

- Cooked basmati rice for serving

DIRECTIONS:

1. In a small glass bowl, whisk together the tomato puree, dark brown sugar, cayenne pepper, dried chives, cinnamon, allspice, crushed thyme, and paprika.

2. Place the pork shoulder in a slow cooker and massage the spice mixture into the pork. Place the carrots and leeks around the pork before pouring the chicken broth into the slow cooker. Sprinkle the ginger over the pork and cook for 5-6 hours on high, or 10 hours on low.

3. When the pork is almost done, place the cilantro, spring onions, pineapple pieces, and bell peppers in a medium bowl and mix to combine. Set the salsa aside.

4. When the pork is done, shred the meat in the slow cooker and season with a pinch of salt and pepper before drizzling with the olive oil. Use a slotted spoon to transfer the pork and carrots to a baking tray. Broil in the oven on high for 5-8 minutes, or until the pork is crispy around the edges. Monitor the heat all the time.

5. Heat the juices from the slow cooker in a pot over medium heat. In a small glass bowl, whisk the corn flour with 2 tbsp. cold water to make a paste. Whisk the corn flour paste into your heated sauce for 3-4 minutes until the sauce thickens.

6. Serve the pulled pork on a bed of cooked rice and top with the thickened gravy and salsa.

GREEK-STYLE LAMB SKEWERS

COOK TIME: 6 MINS | MAKES: 6 SERVINGS

INGREDIENTS:

- ½ tsp. crushed cilantro seeds
- 1 ½ tsp. ground cumin
- 2 tbsp. lemon juice
- 1 tsp. Himalayan salt
- ½ cup garlic-infused olive oil
- ½ cup plain, unsweetened lactose-free yogurt
- Freshly ground black pepper
- 2 lb. boneless leg of lamb, chopped into bite-sized cubes
- 1 green bell pepper, seeded and chopped into bite-sized pieces
- 1 red bell pepper, seeded and chopped into bite-sized pieces
- 2 slender zucchinis, cut into bite-sized rounds
- Avocado oil for greasing

DIRECTIONS:

1. In a large bowl, whisk together the crushed cilantro seeds, ground cumin, lemon juice, salt, garlic-infused olive oil, Greek yogurt, and 1/2 tsp. black pepper. Add the lamb cubes and toss to coat before sealing the bowl and chilling for a minimum of 6 hours.

2. Set the grill in the oven to preheat on medium-high.

3. Begin building your skewers by threading the meat and vegetables onto your skewers, alternating all of the ingredients. (Note: If your vegetables are cut into different sizes, the cooking will be uneven, so make sure that they are all relatively the same size.) Make sure that the ingredients are not touching and leave a few inches at either end of your skewers to serve as handles. Throw out any excess sauce left over in the bowl.

4. Arrange the skewers on a lightly greased baking tray. The skewers should not be touching. Grill the skewers in the oven for about 3 minutes before turning and cooking for an additional 3 minutes.

5. Plate and serve.

ZESTY PAN-FRIED SNAPPER FILLETS

COOK TIME: 25 MINS | MAKES: 4 SERVINGS

INGREDIENTS:

- 2 cups aubergine, thinly sliced
- Sunflower oil
- Flaky sea salt
- Freshly ground black pepper
- 3 cups bok choy, chopped and leaves separated
- 1 ¾ cups zucchinis, sliced into sticks
- 3 tbsp. butter
- ½ cup leeks, thinly sliced (green parts only)
- 16 cherry tomatoes
- 14 oz. snapper fillets
- 3 tsp. lemon peel, grated
- 2 tbsp. lemon juice
- 2 tbsp. parsley, chopped
- Basmati rice, cooked for serving

DIRECTIONS:

1. Toss the aubergine in a large bowl with a drizzle of sunflower oil and season to taste with salt and pepper. Arrange the seasoned aubergine slices on a baking tray and broil in the oven on high for about 4 minutes until fork-tender and golden brown. Set aside.

2. Heat a large skillet over medium-high heat and add enough oil to fry the bok choy stems and zucchini sticks. Toss for 8-10 minutes, or until the vegetables are nicely browned. Add the bok choy leaves to the skillet and season to taste with salt and pepper before frying for an additional 1-2 minutes.

3. Heat a separate skillet over medium-high heat before melting the butter. Once the butter is bubbling, fry the leeks for 1-2 minutes. Stir in the tomatoes before adding the snapper fillets and frying each side for 2-3 minutes.

4. Stir in 2 tsp. grated lemon peel and 1 tsp. lemon juice.

5. Add the aubergine to the skillet and toss to combine.

6. Serve the snapper and vegetables on a bed of basmati rice, topped with the remaining lemon peel, lemon juice, and parsley.

ITALIAN-STYLE BEEF CASSEROLE

COOK TIME: 25 MINS | MAKES: 4 SERVINGS

INGREDIENTS:

- 1 ½ cups chicken broth
- ½ cup uncooked quinoa
- 2 tbsp. garlic-infused olive oil
- 12 oz. lean ground beef
- 2 tsp. low-FODMAP Italian seasoning
- $^1/_3$ cups fresh basil leaves, chopped
- Himalayan salt
- Freshly ground black pepper
- 1 carrot, peeled and diced
- 1 medium red bell pepper, seeded and diced

- ¾ cup cold water
- 6 tbsp. tomato puree
- ¼ cup sweet red wine

DIRECTIONS:

1. Bring the chicken broth and quinoa to a rolling boil in a pot over medium-high heat. Reduce the heat and allow the quinoa to simmer for 15-20 minutes. Set aside.

2. Heat a large frying pan over medium-high heat before adding 1 tbsp. garlic-infused oil. Fry the beef with the lid on for 7-10 minutes, or until the beef is properly cooked. Stir in the remaining olive oil, Italian seasoning, chopped basil, and a pinch of salt and pepper to taste. Allow the flavors to meld for 2-3 minutes before stirring in the carrot and bell pepper.

3. In a separate bowl, whisk together the water and tomato puree before whisking it into the pan along with the other ingredients. Simmer for 3-4 minutes.

4. Whisk in the wine and simmer for an additional 5 minutes before tasting and adjusting the salt and pepper if needed.

5. Gently stir in the cooked quinoa and serve.

SPICY FRIED SHRIMP & BROCCOLI

COOK TIME: 5-10 MINS | MAKES: 6 SERVINGS

INGREDIENTS:

- 1 tsp. brown sugar
- 1 tsp. cayenne pepper
- 1 tsp. corn flour
- 2 tbsp. low-sodium soy sauce
- ½ cup chicken broth
- 2 tbsp. garlic-infused olive oil

- 2 tbsp. fresh ginger, peeled and finely chopped
- 2 cups small broccoli florets
- 1 lb. large shrimp, peeled and deveined
- 2 tsp. toasted sesame oil
- ¼ cup spring onions, chopped (green parts only)

DIRECTIONS:

1. In a medium bowl, whisk together the sugar, cayenne pepper, corn flour, soy sauce, and chicken broth. Set aside while you prepare the rest of the dish.

2. Heat the oil in a large skillet over medium heat and fry the ginger for 1 minute.

3. Turn up the heat and toss in the broccoli for 2 minutes until nicely browned. Add the shrimp and toss for about 30 seconds, or until the shrimp blush.

4. Pour in the stock and stir for about 1 minute, or until the sauce thickens. Remove the skillet from the heat and stir in the sesame oil and spring onions. Plate and serve hot.

BALSAMIC-GLAZED SALMON & SWISS CHARD

COOK TIME: 15 MINS | MAKES: 2 SERVINGS

INGREDIENTS:

- 2 center-cut salmon fillets
- Flaky sea salt
- Freshly ground black pepper
- 1 tsp. dark brown sugar

- 2 tbsp. water
- 3 tbsp. balsamic vinegar
- 1 tbsp. garlic-infused olive oil
- 6 oz. Swiss chard

DIRECTIONS:

1. Allow the salmon fillets to dry on a paper-towel-lined plate before seasoning with a generous pinch of salt and pepper. Set aside.

2. In a small glass bowl, whisk together the sugar, water, and balsamic vinegar.

3. Keep two plates warmed while you prepare the rest of the dish.

4. Heat a large frying pan over medium-high heat before adding 1 tsp. oil and fry the fillets for about 2-4 minutes on each side until the skin is crispy but the middle is not completely cooked. Place the fish in the warmed plates and tent with foil to keep warm.

5. Add the remaining oil to the pan along with the Swiss chard and fry for about 1-2 minutes until the chard just begins to wilt and string throughout (coat the chard in the oil). Place the cooked chard on the plate with the salmon and cover.

6. Whisk the glaze mixture into the hot pan for 30 seconds until it thickens. Immediately pour the glaze over the fillets and serve.

CHEESY CHICKEN ON TOASTED WRAPS

COOK TIME: 25-30 MINS | MAKES: 2 SERVINGS

INGREDIENTS:

- 1 tbsp. garlic-infused olive oil
- ½ medium yellow bell pepper, chopped
- ½ medium green bell pepper, chopped
- ½ medium red bell pepper, chopped
- Himalayan salt
- Freshly ground black pepper
- 1 ½ cups shredded chicken
- 1 tbsp. lime juice
- 2 tbsp. coriander leaves, chopped
- Sunflower oil for frying
- 4 corn wraps

- 3 oz. mozzarella, shredded
- Coriander leaves, chopped for garnish
- Spring onions, chopped (green parts only) for garnish
- Lactose-free sour cream
- 1 cup salsa (I suggest Fody low fodmap salsa)
- 1/8 head iceberg lettuce, shredded

DIRECTIONS:

1. Line a baking pan with tin foil and place a stack of kitchen towels over the foil. Set aside.

2. Heat a large frying pan over medium-high heat before adding the oil and frying the bell peppers for about 5 minutes, or until fork-tender. Season the peppers to taste with a pinch of salt and pepper before pouring them into an oven dish and tenting with foil to keep them warm while you prepare the rest of the dish.

3. In a large bowl, combine the chicken, lime juice, and coriander leaves. Season to taste with salt and pepper, mixing until everything is properly combined.

4. Place the wire rack in the top position of the oven and set the broiler to preheat on high.

5. Wipe the frying pan that you used to cook the peppers before adding about 1" oil. Heat the oil before frying the wraps one at a time (approx. 2 minutes per side, or until the wraps are golden brown). Place the cooked wraps on the tin foil-lined baking pan over the paper towels. Repeat the process with the remaining wraps.

6. Discard the paper towels from the pan. Arrange the wraps on the tin foil-lined sheet. Divide the peppers and chicken between the wraps and top with cheese. Broil in the oven for about 1 minute until the cheese has melted.

7. Place the wraps on plates and garnish with coriander leaves, spring onions, sour cream, salsa, and lettuce before serving.

VEGETARIAN MAINS

STEAMY VEGETABLE TIAN

COOK TIME: 25 MINS | MAKES: 4-6 SERVINGS

INGREDIENTS:

- 4 cups aubergine, chopped into bite-sized pieces
- 2 ½ tsp. flaky sea salt
- 1 tsp. freshly ground black pepper
- 2 tbsp. garlic-infused olive oil
- 2 tbsp. low-FODMAP Italian seasoning
- 3-4 basil leaves, torn in half
- 1 medium zucchini, halved and seeded
- ½ cup red wine
- 1 can tomatoes, diced and drained
- ¼ cup parmesan, shredded
- 1 ½ cups mozzarella, shredded

DIRECTIONS:

1. Pour the chopped aubergine pieces into a colander set over the sink and season with 1 tsp. salt. Allow the aubergine pieces to absorb the salt for 5 minutes before pressing down the pieces with a paper kitchen towel to let out the extra water.

2. Place a large pot over medium-high heat and heat the oil before stirring in the aubergine, Italian seasoning, basil leaves, zucchini halves, 1 ½ tsp. salt, and pepper. Stir until the vegetables are fork-tender (approx. 10 minutes).

3. Stir in the wine for about 2 minutes until most of the liquid has reduced. Add the tomatoes and simmer for an additional 5 minutes.

4. Adjust the seasoning to taste before sprinkling the cheese over the food. Serve when the cheese has melted!

(Tip: Aubergines are low-FODMAP in 1 cup servings while zucchinis are low-FODMAP in servings of $1/3$ cups or less.)

ZESTY AUTUMN RISOTTO

COOK TIME: 45 MINS | MAKES: 4 SERVINGS

INGREDIENTS:

- 2 large carrots, peeled and cut into strips
- 2 cups Japanese pumpkin, peeled and chopped
- 2 tbsp. garlic-infused olive oil
- Himalayan salt
- Freshly ground black pepper
- 1 tbsp. butter
- ½ cup leeks, finely chopped (green parts only)
- 1 ½ cups Arborio rice
- 4 cups low-FODMAP chicken broth, heated
- 4 cups Swiss chard, chopped

- 2 tsp. lemon peel, grated
- 2 ½ tsp. lemon juice
- 2 oz. parmesan, grated
- 2 tbsp. cilantro, chopped

DIRECTIONS:

1. Set the oven to preheat at 400°F. Place a wire rack in the center of the oven.

2. Toss the carrots and pumpkin together on a lightly oiled baking sheet with 1 tbsp. oil. Season with a generous pinch of salt and pepper. Place the sheet in the oven and bake until golden brown and fork-tender (approx. 20-25 minutes), turning the vegetables with a spatula a few times to prevent burning.

3. Place a large pot over medium-high heat before adding the remaining oil and butter to the pot. When the butter is bubbling, fry the leeks for 1-2 minutes until tender. Stir the rice in for 1 minute.

4. Stir in the chicken broth, ½ cup at a time (Note: Wait until all the liquid has been absorbed before adding more). Continue stirring and adding the broth until all the broth has been used. This whole process should take about 20 minutes.

5. Before the last addition of chicken broth, stir in the Swiss chard, grated lemon peel, and lemon juice.

6. Stir in the cheese and top with cilantro before serving.

CHEESY LOW-FODMAP MACARONI

COOK TIME: 20-30 MINS | MAKES: 10-12 SERVINGS

INGREDIENTS:

- 2 ¼ tsp. garlic-infused olive oil
- 1 tsp. butter
- ¾ cups Kellogg's corn flakes, crumbled
- ⅛ tsp. Himalayan salt
- 3 tbsp. parmesan cheese, finely grated

Pasta & Sauce:
- 1 lb. gluten-free tube macaroni
- ½ cup + 1 ½ tsp. cold butter, cubed
- 6 tbsp. gluten-free all-purpose flour

- 4 ½ cups almond milk
- 2 tsp. Himalayan salt
- 1 tsp. freshly ground black pepper
- 1 tbsp. French mustard
- ½ cup parmesan cheese, shredded
- 16 oz. mature cheddar cheese, shredded

DIRECTIONS:

1. With the wire rack in the middle of the oven, set the oven to preheat at 400°F.

2. In a small bowl, crumble the corn flakes with your hands until they resemble breadcrumbs.

3. Heat a large skillet over medium-high heat before adding the oil and butter. When the butter is bubbling, stir in the crumbled corn flake and toss for 1-2 minutes, or until the crumbs are golden brown. Scrape into a bowl and stir in the salt and parmesan. Set aside.

4. Bring a large pot of well-salted water to a rolling boil. When the water is boiling, add the macaroni and cook until just under al dente. Do not make the macaroni too soft, as it will continue to cook in the oven. Pour the cooked macaroni through a colander set over the sink and rinse with cool water. Leave in the colander to drain.

5. Clean the pot before returning it to the heat and melting ½ cup of the butter. Whisk in the flour to form a paste. Continue whisking for about 3 minutes, or until the paste just begins to darken. Gradually pour in the milk while whisking until you have a thick sauce that can coat the back of a wooden spoon (approx. 3 minutes).

6. Transfer the pot to a wooden chopping board and whisk in the salt, pepper, and French mustard. Use a wooden spoon to stir in the parmesan and cheddar until all of the cheese has melted (Note: The sauce should still be hot enough to melt the cheese; returning the sauce to the heat to melt the cheese faster may result in the sauce being less creamy).

7. Coat the inside of an ovenproof casserole dish with the rest of the butter. Add the cooked macaroni to the pot with the cheese sauce and mix until everything is properly combined. Scrape the cheesy macaroni into the buttered casserole dish and bake in the oven for 18-20 minutes, or until the top is golden brown. If it looks like the macaroni is cooking too fast, cover the top with tin foil and continue baking.

8. Serve straight away.

QUINOA & RICE KHICHRI

COOK TIME: 28 MINS | MAKES: 4 SERVINGS

INGREDIENTS:

- ½ red bell pepper, chopped
- 1 carrot, peeled and diced
- 2 cups low-FODMAP vegetable broth
- 1 cup uncooked quinoa
- 1 tsp. turmeric powder
- ½ tsp. ground cumin
- 1 cup brown rice, cooked
- ¼ cup parsley, chopped
- 2 tbsp. garlic-infused olive oil
- Himalayan salt
- Freshly ground black pepper

DIRECTIONS:

1. In a large saucepan over medium-high heat, combine the red pepper, carrot, vegetable broth, quinoa, turmeric, and cumin. Allow the quinoa to simmer until most of the liquid has reduced (approx. 25 minutes. You should have a thin sauce – add extra broth if needed.

2. Add the lentils, parsley, and garlic-infused oil. Stir for about 2-3 minutes, or until everything is properly combined and heated.

3. Season to taste with salt and pepper. Serve hot.

ITALIAN HERB-STYLE RIBBON PASTA

COOK TIME: 25-30 MINS| MAKES: 4 SERVINGS

INGREDIENTS:

- Sea salt
- 12 oz. gluten-free ribbon pasta
- ¼ cup garlic-infused olive oil
- 1 cup fresh parsley, chopped
- 8 oz. canned fire-roasted red peppers, seeded and chopped
- Freshly ground black pepper

DIRECTIONS:

1. Fill a large pot with salted water and bring to a boil over medium-high heat. Remember that when you are making pasta, you want the water to be as salty as the sea. When the water has reached a rolling boil, add the pasta and cook until al dente, stirring a few times throughout to prevent sticking.

2. Pour the cooked pasta through a colander set over the sink and allow to drain.

3. Transfer the drained pasta to a large serving dish and gently fold in the oil, parsley, and red peppers. Season to taste with salt and pepper before serving.

POTATO CURRY IN COCONUT MILK

COOK TIME: 20 MINS | MAKES: 7 SERVINGS

INGREDIENTS:

- 2 tbsp. garlic-infused olive oil
- 1 tbsp. fresh ginger, peeled and crushed
- 1 cup carrots, peeled and chopped
- 1 tsp. ground cumin
- 2 tsp. turmeric powder
- 28 oz. canned tomatoes

- 1 cup raw quinoa
- 3 cups low-FODMAP vegetable broth
- ½ cup unsweetened coconut milk
- 1 ½ cups waxy potatoes, boiled and cubed
- Kosher salt
- Freshly ground black pepper

DIRECTIONS:

1. Heat a large cast-iron pot over medium heat before adding the oil, ginger, and chopped carrots. Fry for 5-10 minutes until the carrots are tender.

2. Add the cumin and turmeric powder. Stir and allow the flavors to meld for 1-2 minutes.

3. Stir in the tomatoes, quinoa, and vegetable broth. Simmer until the quinoa softens (approx. 15 minutes).

4. Add the coconut milk and cubed potatoes. Stir for 1-2 minutes until the potatoes are heated through.

5. Add a pinch of salt and pepper to taste before serving

(Tip: Canned tomatoes are low-FODMAP at 4 oz. servings.)

CHEESY SWISS CHARD WRAPS

COOK TIME: 15 MINS | MAKES: 8 SERVINGS

INGREDIENTS:

- 1 tbsp. garlic-infused olive oil
- 8 oz. Swiss chard, rinsed and chopped
- 8 soft corn wraps (big enough to comfortably fit in a pan)

- 2 cups baby tomatoes, halved
- 2 cups mozzarella cheese, shredded

DIRECTIONS:

1. Heat a large fry pan over medium-high heat before adding the oil and tossing the Swiss chard for 5 minutes, or until it has reduced in size by half. Scrape the cooked chard into a dish and keep warm while you prepare the rest of the dish.

2. Return the pan to the heat and add one wrap. Top the wrap with ¼ of the tomato halves, followed by a generous amount of the cooked chard. Then top with cheese. Cover the cheese with a second wrap and use a pot or spatula to press it down into the pan. Place the lid on the pan and cook the wraps for 6 minutes, flipping halfway through. The wraps should be nicely toasted on both sides. Repeat the process with the remaining wraps and ingredients.

3. Place the cooked wraps on a serving platter and slice before serving.

(Tip: Corn wraps are naturally low-FODMAP.)

TEMPEH & CHARD ON BROWN RICE

COOK TIME: 5-10 MINS | MAKES: 4 SERVINGS

INGREDIENTS:

- 14-16 oz. extra-firm tempeh
- 1 tbsp. rice vinegar
- 1 tbsp. toasted sesame oil
- 3 tbsp. tamari sauce
- 2 tbsp. garlic-infused olive oil
- 1 tbsp. fresh ginger, finely shredded
- 3 tbsp. spring onions, chopped (green parts only)

- 2 ½ cups bok choy, cleaned and chopped
- 8 oz. Swiss chard, cleaned and chopped
- Long-grain brown rice, cooked to serve

DIRECTIONS:

1. Press your tempeh by placing it in a single layer between two stacks of paper kitchen towels and weighing it down with something heavy like a pile of books placed on a baking tray. Allow the tempeh to be pressed for roughly 10 minutes.

2. Meanwhile, in a small glass bowl, whisk together the rice vinegar, toasted sesame oil, and tamari sauce. Set aside on the counter while you chop the pressed tempeh into 1 ½" squares.

3. Heat a large frypan over medium-high heat before adding 1 tbsp. oil. When the oil is piping hot, fry the tempeh in batches for a couple of minutes, or until the tempeh squares are nicely toasted on all sides. Arrange the cooked tempeh squares on a plate and used a basting brush to marinate the squares in the prepared tamari sauce.

4. Return the pan to the heat and add the remaining 1 tbsp. oil. Toss in the ginger and spring onions for about 1 minute. Toss in the Bok choy for about 30 seconds until everything is properly combined before adding the Swiss chard and half of the tamari sauce. Stir the chard for an additional 1-2 minutes until it has reduced in size. The bok choy should be tender while still crispy around the edges. Add the rest of the sauce along with the tempeh and carefully stir until the tempeh is heated through.

5. Serve the tempeh and vegetables on a bed of cooked brown rice.

TEMPEH & PASTA WITH PESTO SAUCE

COOK TIME: 20 MINS | MAKES: 6 SERVINGS

INGREDIENTS:

- 4 cups spinach, cleaned and chopped
- ½ small lemon, juiced
- 1 tbsp. nutritional yeast
- 1 cup fresh basil leaves
- ¼ cup toasted walnuts, chopped
- Kosher salt
- Freshly ground black pepper
- 6 tbsp. garlic-infused olive oil
- 12 oz. gluten-free fusilli
- 1 ½ tsp. avocado oil

- 14 oz. extra-firm tempeh, drained and cut into 1 ½" squares
- 1 tbsp. low-sodium soy sauce

DIRECTIONS:

1. Pulse the spinach in a food processor until fine (approx. 20-30 seconds). Add the lemon juice, nutritional yeast, basil leaves, and walnuts. Pulse for a few seconds before seasoning to taste with salt and pepper.

2. With the food processor pulsing, gradually pour in the oil and continue to pulse until you have a thick sauce. Taste and adjust the salt and pepper if desired. Set aside while you prepare the rest of the dish.

3. Bring a large pot of salty water to a rolling boil over high heat before adding the fusilli. Cook until just under al dente. Drain the cooked fusilli before returning it to the pot and stirring in ½ tsp. avocado oil.

4. Heat a large skillet over medium-high heat before adding the remaining avocado oil along with the soy sauce and tempeh. Toss and fry the tempeh squares for about 20 minutes until golden brown on all sides.

5. Fold the tempeh and pesto sauce into the pot of cooked pasta.

6. Scrape into a serving dish and serve hot.

CHEESY LOW-FODMAP VEGETABLE SOUP

COOK TIME: 1 HOUR | MAKES: 10-12 SERVINGS

INGREDIENTS:

- 3 tbsp. garlic-infused olive oil
- 1 cup leeks, chopped (green parts only)
- 1 tsp. Himalayan salt
- 4 oz. parmesan rind
- 1 can fire-roasted diced tomatoes
- 10 cups vegetable stock
- 1 bay leaf, torn
- 2 thyme sprigs
- 6 parsley sprigs
- 6 black peppercorns
- 1 fennel bulb, thinly sliced
- 2 turnips, thinly sliced
- 2 parsnips, peeled and thinly sliced
- 2 carrots, peeled and sliced into thin rounds
- 3 russet potatoes, peeled and cut into bite-sized pieces
- 2 zucchinis, trimmed and sliced
- 2 medium yellow summer squash, trimmed and sliced
- 1 large bunch spinach, cleaned and chopped
- Freshly ground black pepper
- Parmesan, grated for sprinkling

DIRECTIONS:

1. Heat a large cast-iron pot over medium heat before adding the oil. When the oil is hot, stir in the leeks for about 5 minutes until tender.

2. Stir in ½ tsp. salt, the parmesan rind, diced tomatoes, vegetable stock, bay leaves, thyme sprigs, parsley, peppercorns, fennel bulb, turnips, parsnips, carrots, and potatoes. Bring to a rolling boil before reducing the heat. Allow the soup to simmer with the lid on until the vegetables are tender (approx. 30-40 minutes). Stir the soup every 5-10 minutes to prevent burning.

3. Stir in the zucchinis, summer squash, and spinach. Continue to simmer the soup until all the vegetables are tender (approx. 2o minutes). Taste the soup and season to taste with the remaining salt and a pinch of freshly ground black pepper if needed.

4. Ladle the soup into bowls and serve with a generous sprinkling of parmesan.

STIR-FRY & PEANUT SAUCE

COOK TIME: 20 MINS | MAKES: 3 SERVINGS

INGREDIENTS:

- 1 tsp. fresh ginger, grated
- 1 tsp. tabasco sauce (optional)
- 1 tbsp. light corn syrup
- 1 tbsp. rice vinegar
- ½ lime, juiced
- 3 tbsp. smooth natural peanut butter
- 3 tbsp. dark brown sugar
- 1 tbsp. low-sodium soy sauce

- ¼ cup canola oil
- 1 tsp. garlic-infused olive oil
- 12 oz. extra-firm tempeh, drained and cubed
- 1 extra-large free-range egg, scrambled
- ½ cup bean sprouts
- Fresh cilantro, chopped for garnish
- Roasted peanuts, chopped for garnish

DIRECTIONS:

1. In a medium glass bowl, whisk together the ginger, tabasco, corn syrup, rice vinegar, lime juice, peanut butter, dark brown sugar, soy sauce, and canola oil. Set aside while you prepare the rest of the dish.

2. Fill a large pot with salted water and bring to a rolling boil. When the water is boiling, cook the noodles until just soft. Drain the water, leaving the noodles behind.

3. Heat a large wok over medium-high heat before adding the oil. When the oil is hot, fry the tempeh for about 5 minutes until evenly browned. Shift the tempeh to the side and gently scrambled the egg until properly cooked.

4. Toss the noodles into the wok along with the peanut sauce and cook for about 5 minutes, or until the peanut sauce thickens. Gently fold in the bean sprouts.

5. Plate the stir-fry and garnish with the cilantro and peanuts before serving.

(Tips: Beansprouts are extremely low-FODMAP and can be enjoyed in large amounts.)

FRESH VEGETABLE LINGUINE

COOK TIME: 15 MINS | MAKES: 4 SERVINGS

INGREDIENTS:

- 1 tbsp. garlic-infused olive oil
- 1 cup leeks, finely chopped (green leaves only)
- 1 dried bay leaf
- 1 tsp. brown sugar
- 4 cups Swiss chard, chopped
- 1 red bell pepper, sliced
- 1 ½ cups low-FODMAP vegetable broth
- 1 ½ tbsp. tomato paste
- 1 can crushed tomatoes
- Kosher salt
- Freshly ground black pepper
- 1 tsp. corn flour

- 2 tbsp. water
- 4 tbsp. sunflower seeds
- ½ lb. gluten-free linguini, cooked for serving
- ½ cup mozzarella, grated

DIRECTIONS:

1. Add the oil to a medium saucepan and heat over medium heat before frying the leeks until tender (approx. 2-3 minutes). Stir in the bay leaf, brown sugar, chard, red pepper, vegetable broth, crushed tomatoes, and tomato paste. Simmer for 15 minutes, stirring occasionally. After 15 minutes, season to taste with salt and pepper.

2. In a small glass bowl, whisk the corn flour with 2 tbsp. cold water to form a paste. Whisk the corn flour paste into the pot. Stir for 1-2 minutes, or until the sauce thickens. Discard the bay leaf.

3. Dry-roast the sunflower seeds over medium-high heat until nicely browned (approx. 2-3 minutes). Set aside off the heat.

4. Toss in the greens and sauce with the linguine and serve topped with the roasted sunflower seeds and mozzarella.

SIDES

VEGETARIAN PILAF

COOK TIME: 25 MINS | MAKES: 8 SERVINGS

INGREDIENTS:

- 4 cups low-FODMAP vegetable broth
- 2 tsp. garlic-infused olive oil
- 2 cups long-grain brown rice
- ½ cup fresh parsley, chopped
- Kosher salt
- Freshly ground black pepper

DIRECTIONS:

1. Place the vegetable broth in a large pot over low heat with the lid on.

2. While the broth is heating, place a large frypan over medium-high heat and heat the oil. When the oil is hot, add the uncooked rice and toast for a few minutes until nicely browned. Toss occasionally.

3. Scrape the browned rice into the pot with the warmed stock and reduce the heat. Simmer the rice and stock for 15-25 minutes, or until the rice is properly cooked. Transfer the pot to a wooden chopping board and allow the rice to rest with the lid on the pot for 10 minutes.

4. Taste the rice and season with salt and pepper if necessary.

5. Gently fold in the parsley and serve.

(Tip: Cooked rice can be enjoyed in 1 cup servings as it is naturally low-FODMAP.)

TANGY VEGETABLE SALAD

COOK TIME: 0 MINS | MAKES: 24 SERVINGS

INGREDIENTS:

Vinaigrette:
- 1 tsp. French mustard
- 3 tbsp. red wine vinegar
- 6 tbsp. extra-virgin olive oil
- Himalayan salt
- Freshly ground black pepper

Salad:
- ¾ cups toasted almond slivers
- ¾ cups toasted pumpkin seeds
- 3 cups crumbled feta cheese
- ¼ cup parsley, finely chopped
- ½ cup spring onions, chopped (green parts only)
- 3 medium carrots, peeled and julienned

- 6 oz. green beans, chopped
- 1 celery root, trimmed and diced
- 1 cup cherry tomatoes, halved
- 3 different color bell peppers, seeded and diced
- 1 medium cucumber, sliced into thin rounds
- 1 cup red cabbage, chopped
- 1 whole bok choy, diced
- 2 cups romaine lettuce, chopped
- 2 cups kale, chopped

DIRECTIONS:

1. In a small glass bowl, whisk together the mustard and red wine vinegar. While whisking briskly, drizzle in the olive oil. Season to taste with salt and pepper, if desired, and whisk until everything is properly combined. Set aside.

2. In a large bowl, combine the almonds, pumpkin seeds, feta, parsley, spring onions, carrots, green beans, celery root, tomatoes, bell peppers, cucumber, red cabbage, bok choy, lettuce, and cabbage. Toss to combine.

3. Drizzle the salad with just enough of the dressing to coat all of the vegetables in a light layer. Serve straight away.

(Tip: The salad can be made ahead of time and refrigerated for up to 3 days in an airtight container – simply omit the nuts, cheese, and dressing until you are ready to serve the salad.)

EGGY POTATO SALAD

COOK TIME: 25 MINS | MAKES: 4 SERVINGS

INGREDIENTS:

- Sea salt
- 1 ¾ lb. Yukon gold potatoes, peeled and cubed
- 1 ¼ cups green beans, chopped
- 4 large free-range eggs
- 1 tbsp. lemon juice
- $1/_3$ cup mayonnaise
- 1 tbsp. whole grain mustard
- Freshly ground black pepper
- 1 red bell pepper, seeded and diced
- 1 small English cucumber, peeled and chopped
- 3 tbsp. spring onions, finely chopped (green parts only)
- 3 tbsp. fresh chives, finely chopped

DIRECTIONS:

1. Place the potatoes in a pot of well-salted water and bring to a boil. Cook the potatoes until the cubes are fork-tender. Just before you remove the potatoes from the pot, blanch the green beans for about 3 minutes in the hot water until the color brightens. Pour the cooked potatoes and green beans through a colander set over the sink and allow to drain while you prepare the rest of the meal.

2. Fill a small pot with water and bring to a rolling boil. Once the water is boiling, carefully lower the eggs into the pot using a slotted spoon. Boil the eggs for about 8-10 minutes before removing the pot from the heat and running the eggs under cold water. This will stop the cooking process. Peel the eggs and roughly chop them before placing them in a large bowl.

3. In a small glass bowl, whisk together the lemon juice, vegan mayonnaise, and mustard. Season to taste with a generous pinch of black pepper. Set aside.

4. Add the bell pepper, cucumber, spring onions, and chives to the bowl with the chopped eggs and gently toss. Carefully toss in the cooked potatoes, blanched green beans, and the mustard dressing. Carefully mix until everything is just combined – do not over mix.

5. Season with extra salt and pepper if necessary and serve.

ROASTED GARLIC FRENCH FRIES

COOK TIME: 25 MINS | MAKES: 4 SERVINGS

INGREDIENTS:

- 2 tbsp. avocado oil
- 2 tbsp. garlic-infused olive oil
- 1 ½ lb. Yukon gold potatoes, scrubbed and patted dry
- Flaky sea salt

DIRECTIONS:

1. Cover two baking sheets with greaseproof paper that has been coated with an extra layer of baking spray and set the oven to preheat at 450°F with two wire rack in the lower and upper thirds of the oven.

2. In a small glass bowl, whisk together the avocado oil and garlic-infused olive oil. Set aside.

3. Slice the dry potatoes into long strips for French fries. Arrange the fries on the prepared baking sheet in a single layer, leaving about ½" between the fries to ensure crisp cooking. Drizzle half of the oil over all of the fries and season generously with the flaky sea salt.

4. Roast the fries in the oven for 10-15 minutes, switching the sheets halfway through the cooking time.

5. Remove the sheets from the oven and flip the fries. Use the remaining oil to drizzle the fries and season with more salt before returning the sheets to the oven for an additional 10 minutes. The fries should be golden brown when done.

6. Serve hot.

GARDEN SALAD WITH ITALIAN DRESSING

COOK TIME: 0 MINS | MAKES: 6 SERVINGS

INGREDIENTS:

Italian Dressing:
- 1 tsp. brown sugar
- ¼ tsp. cayenne pepper
- ½ tsp. crushed basil
- ¾ tsp. dried oregano
- ½ tsp. kosher salt
- ½ tsp. freshly ground black pepper
- 2 tsp. garlic-infused olive oil
- 3 ½ tsp. red wine vinegar
- ¾ cup extra-virgin olive oil

Salad:
- 2 cups cooked chicken, shredded
- 1 red bell pepper, seeded and diced
- 2 radishes, thinly sliced
- 1 small English cucumber, chopped
- 1 cup cherry tomatoes, halved
- 5-6 cups assorted lettuce leaves

DIRECTIONS:

1. In a glass bowl, whisk together the brown sugar, cayenne pepper, crushed basil, oregano, salt, black pepper, garlic-infused olive oil, red wine vinegar, and extra-virgin olive oil. Set aside on the counter for 30 minutes before using, or store in the fridge in a glass bottle for up to 3 weeks. (Note: You may need to let the dressing warm on the counter after it has been stored in the fridge.)

2. In a large bowl, toss together the chicken, bell pepper, radishes, cucumber, tomatoes, and assorted lettuce leaves. Drizzle the salad with just enough of the dressing to coat all of the ingredients and serve.

(Tip: Store-bought salad dressing may contain ingredients that are high-FODMAP.)

BAKED AUBERGINE & ZUCCHINIS

COOK TIME: 40-60 MINS | MAKES: 6 SERVINGS

INGREDIENTS:

- 2 small zucchinis, trimmed
- 1 large aubergine, ends trimmed
- 2 medium Yukon gold potatoes, scrubbed
- 3 medium heirloom tomatoes
- ¼ cup garlic-infused olive oil
- 3-4 fresh rosemary sprigs
- Himalayan salt
- freshly ground black pepper

DIRECTIONS:

1. Set the oven to preheat at 400°F with the wire rack in the middle of the oven.

2. Prep all the vegetables by slicing them into ⅛" rounds. The zucchinis, aubergine, potatoes, and tomatoes can either be sliced into rounds or cut into thin strips.

3. Use a basting brush to coat the inside of a large oven-proof dish – make sure to coat the edges of the dish as well. Begin layering the vegetables in overlapping layers, or in any other design of your choice (e.g., concentric circles). Use the basting brush to coat the tops of the vegetables with oil and season with a generous amount of salt and pepper. Place the rosemary sprigs on top.

4. Place the dish in the oven and bake for about 40-60 minutes, or until the vegetables are all fork-tender. If the vegetables start to burn, you can cover the dish with tin foil and continue baking until cooked.

5. Remove the dish from the oven and serve immediately.

CREAMY TURMERIC SWEET POTATO SALAD

COOK TIME: 15 MINS | MAKES: 8 SERVINGS

INGREDIENTS:

- 6 oz. extra-firm tempeh, drained and cubed
- 1 tbsp. soy sauce
- 15 oz. sweet potato, cooked
- 1 tsp. turmeric powder
- 5 tbsp. low fodmap mayonnaise
- Himalayan salt
- Freshly ground black pepper
- ¼ cup toasted almond slivers
- 2 tbsp. chives, chopped
- ¾ cups red grapes, halved

DIRECTIONS:

1. Cover a baking pan with tin foil and set the oven to preheat at 350°F with the wire rack in the middle of the oven.

2. Arrange the tempeh cubes on your prepared baking sheet and baste them with the soy sauce. Allow the cubes to rest for 5 minutes before placing the tray in the oven and baking for about 15 minutes.

3. Mash the cooked sweet potato in a large bowl before adding the turmeric powder and mayonnaise. Stir until everything is properly combined and season to taste with salt and pepper. Set aside.

4. When the tempeh is cool enough to work with, crumble it into the bowl of sweet potato and stir in the almond slivers, chives, and red grapes.

(Tips: Grapes are fantastically low-FODMAP and can be enjoyed in large amounts.)

CHEESY CHICKEN SALAD

COOK TIME: 12-15 MINS | MAKES: 4 SERVINGS

INGREDIENTS:

- ¼ tsp. Worcestershire sauce
- ½ tsp. French mustard
- 1 tbsp. lemon juice
- 2 tbsp. garlic-infused olive oil
- 1 tbsp. parmesan cheese
- 4 oil-packed canned anchovy fillets (reserve 1 tsp. oil)
- Himalayan salt
- Freshly ground black pepper
- 2 tbsp. avocado oil
- ½ cup parmesan, grated
- ½ cup cornflakes, crumbled
- 4 boneless chicken breasts with the skin removed
- 2 large heads romaine lettuce
- 2 tbsp. fresh parsley, chopped

DIRECTIONS:

1. In a medium glass bowl, whisk together the Worcester sauce, French mustard, lemon juice, and garlic-infused olive oil before stirring in the parmesan and anchovies. Stir until everything is properly combined. Taste and add a pinch of salt and pepper if needed.

2. Set the oven to preheat at 450°F with the wire rack in the middle of the oven.

3. In a separate bowl, whisk together the reserved anchovy oil, avocado oil, parmesan, and crumbled corn flakes. Season to taste with salt and pepper.

4. Arrange the chicken breasts on half of a baking sheet. Quarter the lettuce heads and arrange them on the other half. Use half of the mustard dressing to baste the lettuce heads and pack the breadcrumbs on top of the chicken fillets in a single layer.

5. Place the sheet in the oven and bake until the chicken is properly cooked (approx. 12-15 minutes).

6. Remove the sheet from the oven and allow the chicken to cool for 5 minutes on the counter.

7. Arrange the cooked chicken and lettuce on a serving platter. Drizzle the remaining dressing over the chicken and lettuce before decorating with the parsley. Serve.

DESSERTS

DECADENT PECAN CRUMBLE CAKE

COOK TIME: 1 ½ HOURS | MAKES: 14-16 SERVINGS

INGREDIENTS:

For the crumble:
- ½ cup butter, cubed
- ½ tsp. Kosher salt
- 1 tbsp. ground cinnamon
- ½ tsp. ground nutmeg
- ¾ cup dark brown sugar
- ½ cup lightly toasted pecans, roughly chopped
- 1 cup gluten-free all-purpose flour

For the cake:
- ½ tsp. Kosher salt
- 1 ½ tsp. bicarbonate of soda

- 1 ½ tsp. baking powder
- 3 cups gluten-free all-purpose flour
- 1 ½ cups butter
- 1 ½ cups granulated brown sugar
- 3 large free-range eggs
- 2 ¼ tsp. pure vanilla essence
- 1 ½ cups lactose-free sour cream

For the glaze:
- 1 tbsp. water
- 1 cup icing sugar, sifted

DIRECTIONS:

1. Set the oven to preheat at 325°F with the wire rack in the middle of the oven. Spray and flour a round or shaped cake tin.

2. Melt the butter in a microwave-safe bowl, or on the stove. Scrape the melted butter into a large bowl. Beat in the salt, cinnamon, nutmeg, and brown sugar until properly combined – the sugar should be light and airy.

3. Fold in the toasted nuts and flour. Beak the mixture up using your fingers until you have a mixture that resembles coarse sand.

4. In a large bowl, whisk together the salt, bicarbonate of soda, baking powder, and flour.

5. In a separate bowl, beat the butter and sugar until light and frothy, incorporating as much air as possible. Add the eggs and vanilla, beating until properly combined.

6. With the mixer running on low, alternate between the flour mixture and sour cream, scraping the bowl down with every addition until all of the ingredients are properly combined.

7. Scrape half of the batter into your prepared cake tin and smooth out the top. Top with half of the pecan crumb mixture. Carefully pour the remaining batter over the crumbs and smooth out the surface. Sprinkle the remaining crumbs over the top. Gently push the crumbs down into the cake so that they stick.

8. Place the cake tin in the oven for 55-65 minutes, or until the top is nicely browned and an inserted toothpick comes out clean. Place the cake tin on a wire rack for 20 minutes to cool before turning it out onto a cake platter.

9. Place the water and icing sugar in a small pot and whisk until just combined. Heat the icing and water for about 15 seconds over low heat – you want the icing to melt but not get too hot. When the icing is completely melted, drizzle it over the cooled cake and serve.

CHOCOLATE CHIP KELLOGG'S COOKIES

COOK TIME: 10 MINS | MAKES: 20 SERVINGS

INGREDIENTS:

- ½ cup almond butter
- ½ cup light corn syrup
- ½ cup light brown sugar
- ½ tsp. pure vanilla essence
- ½ cup semi-sweet chocolate chips
- 2 cups low-FODMAP Kellogg's cornflakes

DIRECTIONS:

1. Cover a baking pan with greaseproof paper and set aside.

2. In a saucepan, whisk together the butter, corn syrup, and brown sugar over medium-low heat until the sugar granules melt. As soon as the sugar begins to bubble, transfer the saucepan to a wooden chopping board and whisk in the vanilla essence. Carefully fold in the cornflakes until evenly coated in the melted sugar. Add the chocolate chips and stir until properly combined.

3. Working quickly so as not to let the mixture harden, use an ice cream scoop to dollop large balls onto the prepared baking pan.

4. Allow the cookies to harden on the counter, or chill in the fridge until ready to serve.

(Tips: Although corn flakes are low-FODMAP, they are not gluten-free and should be substituted when avoiding gluten. While regular corn syrup is low-FODMAP, high fructose corn syrup is not and should be avoided.)

CHOCOLATE-DRIZZLED RASPBERRY MUFFINS

COOK TIME: 20 MINS | MAKES: 12 MUFFINS

INGREDIENTS:

- 6 tbsp. butter, cubed
- 2 ½ cups gluten-free self-rising flour
- ½ cup dark chocolate, roughly chopped
- 1 cup raspberries
- 1 cup almond milk
- 1 tsp. chia seeds, soaked in 2 tbsp. water
- Icing sugar for dusting

DIRECTIONS:

1. Generously butter a muffin tin and set the oven to preheat at 375°F with the wire rack in the middle of the oven.

2. In a large bowl, combine the butter and flour – use your hands to rub the mixture together until it resembles coarse sand. Add the chocolate, raspberries, almond milk, and soaked chia seeds. Fold until everything is just combined.

3. Spoon the batter into the prepared muffin tin in even amounts and bake in the oven for 15-20 minutes, or until the tops are golden and an inserted toothpick comes out clean. (Note: There may still be melted chocolate on the toothpick.)

4. Allow the muffins to cool in the tin for 5 minutes before transferring them to a cooling rack. Dust with icing sugar when slightly cooled and serve warm..

PECAN & BUTTERSCOTCH BROWNIES

COOK TIME: 20-25 MINS | MAKES: 25 BARS

INGREDIENTS:

- 1 tsp. gluten-free baking powder
- ¼ tsp. Kosher salt
- 1 ¼: cups gluten-free all-purpose flour
- 1/3 cup toasted pecans, roughly chopped
- 6 oz. dark chocolate, roughly chopped
- ½ cup butter, cubed
- 1 ½ tsp. pure vanilla essence
- 1 cup dark brown sugar
- 1 large free-range egg

DIRECTIONS:

1. Set the oven to preheat at 350°F with the wire rack in the center of the oven. Spray a baking sheet with baking spray and set it aside.

2. In a large bowl, whisk together the baking powder, salt, and flour before folding in the pecans and chocolate.

3. In a medium pot over medium heat, melt the butter until the milk solids separate and brown – you want a nice golden toast, so make sure that the butter does not burn. Once the butter is nice and brown, scrape it into a large mixing bowl and set aside on the counter to cool. You want it cool enough to touch but not so cool that the butter begins to solidify again. Beat in the vanilla essence and sugar, followed by the egg when the sugar is light and fluffy.

4. Fold in the flour mixture until all the ingredients just come together in a batter. Scrape the batter onto the prepared sheet and smooth out the top with an offset spatula.

5. Place the sheet in the oven until the top is golden brown and the edges are nice and crispy (approx. 20-25 minutes).

6. Leave the brownies to cool completely on the sheet before slicing and serving. Store in an airtight container for up to 3 days with greaseproof paper between each brownie.

RICH WALNUT BROWNIES

COOK TIME: 10 MINS | MAKES: 24 BROWNIES

INGREDIENTS:

- ⅛ tsp. Himalayan salt
- 1 cup pure cocoa powder
- 2 ½ cups icing sugar
- 3 egg whites (more if needed)
- 1 cup toasted walnuts, roughly chopped
- 2 tsp. pure vanilla essence

DIRECTIONS:

1. Line a baking pan with greaseproof paper and set the oven to preheat at 350°F with the wire rack in the middle of the oven.

2. Whisk the salt, cocoa powder, and icing sugar together in a large bowl – incorporate as much air as possible while whisking.

3. Gently fold in the egg whites using a wooden spoon – you want a thick dough, so add more whites if needed so as to get the right consistency – before folding in the nuts and vanilla essence.

4. Use an ice cream scoop to arrange balls of the batter onto the prepared baking pan (approx. 2" apart). Place the sheet in the oven until the brownies crack and set (approx. 10 minutes).

5. Allow the brownies to cool on the pan before serving.

(Tip: Walnuts can be enjoyed in low-FODMAP servings of ¼ cups.)

SIMPLE BLUEBERRY TART

COOK TIME: 30 MINS | MAKES: 15 SERVINGS

INGREDIENTS:

- ½ tsp. ground cinnamon
- ⅓ tsp. ground nutmeg
- ¼ tsp. Kosher salt
- 3 cups gluten-free self-rising flour
- ¾ cups light brown sugar
- ½ lb. butter, softened
- 1 large free-range egg
- 3 cups blueberries
- ¼ cup brown sugar
- 3 tsp. corn flour

DIRECTIONS:

1. Set the oven to preheat at 350°F with the wire rack in the middle of the oven. Line a large-rimmed baking sheet with greaseproof paper.

2. In a large bowl, whisk together the cinnamon, nutmeg, salt, flour, and sugar to incorporate as much air as possible.

3. In a small bowl, beat the softened butter and egg until light and foamy.

4. Use a wooden spoon to fold the butter and egg into the flour mixture. When the ingredients come together, use your hands to work the crumbs into coarse sand.

5. Transfer half of the crumb mixture to the prepared sheet and use the bottom of a glass to tightly press it down. Arrange the blueberries over the crumbs in an even layer.

6. In a small glass bowl, whisk together the sugar and corn flour before sprinkling it over the layer of blueberries. Top the tart with the remaining crumbs.

7. Bake the tart in the oven until nicely browned (approx. 30 minutes). Remove the sheet from the oven and allow the tart to cool completely before slicing and serving.

LOW-FODMAP CHOCOLATE PUDDING

COOK TIME: 5-10 MINS | MAKES: 8 SERVINGS

INGREDIENTS:

- ½ tsp. Himalayan salt
- 2 tbsp. corn flour
- $1/3$ cup brown sugar
- $1/3$ cup pure cocoa powder, sifted
- 2 cups lactose free milk
- 4 oz. dark chocolate, roughly chopped
- 1 tsp. pure vanilla essence
- Whipped cream for serving

DIRECTIONS:

1. Line up 8 dessert bowls on the counter – you want them ready as soon as the pudding is done.
2. In a medium pot, whisk together the salt, corn flour, brown sugar, and cocoa powder. Whisk in 1 cup of the almond milk to form a paste before gradually whisking in the remaining cup.
3. Place the pot over medium heat and bring to a simmer while whisking. Once the mixture is simmering, whisk continuously until the mixture thickens. Whisk in the chopped chocolate until everything has melted (approx. 1 additional minute).
4. When the pudding is thick enough to form rivulets on the surface, transfer the pot to a wooden chopping board and briskly whisk in the vanilla essence.
5. Divide the pudding between the bowls and chill in the fridge once the pudding has cooled to room temperature.
6. The pudding is ready when the top is set and jiggly. Serve with a large dollop of whipped cream on each pudding.

(Tip: whipped cream is low-FODMAP and can be enjoyed in moderation , up to a ½ cup serving.)

SIMPLE CARROT MUG MUFFIN

COOK TIME: 2-3 MINS | MAKES: 2 SERVINGS

INGREDIENTS:

- 1 large free-range egg
- ¼ cup brown sugar (more for garnish)
- 3 tbsp. carrot, shredded
- ½ tsp. ground cinnamon (more for garnish)
- ⅛ tsp. baking powder
- ⅛ tsp. xanthan gum
- ¼ tsp. salt
- 5 tbsp. gluten-free all-purpose flour
- ½ tsp. pure vanilla essence
- 2 tbsp. almond milk
- 1 tbsp. coconut, shredded
- 1 tbsp. toasted walnuts, roughly chopped

DIRECTIONS:

1. In a small bowl, whisk the egg until light and frothy. Transfer 2 tbsp. to a microwave-safe mug. The remaining egg can be refrigerated for another use, or thrown away.

2. Briskly whisk in the oil before stirring in the carrots.

3. In a separate bowl, whisk together the cinnamon, baking powder, xanthan gum, Kosher salt, and flour – incorporate as much air as possible. Beat the flour mixture into the mug until properly combined before beating in the vanilla and milk. Gently stir in the shredded coconut and walnuts.

4. Garnish the top with extra sugar and cinnamon before placing the mug in the microwave for just over 2 minutes. Make sure that the muffin does not spill over the sides.

5. Serve straight away and enjoy!

(Tip: Carrots are naturally low-FODMAP and can be enjoyed in large amounts.)

DECADENT BUTTERSCOTCH & BANANA DESSERT

COOK TIME: 45 MINS | MAKES: 6 SERVINGS

INGREDIENTS:

- 3 tsp. gluten-free baking powder
- 1 ½ cups gluten-free all-purpose flour
- 6 tbsp. butter
- ½ cup lactose free milk
- 1 tsp. pure vanilla extract
- 1 large free-range egg, beaten
- 1 cup unripe banana, mashed
- 1 tbsp. corn flour
- ½ cup dark brown sugar
- 2 tbsp. pure maple syrup
- 1 tbsp. dark molasses
- 2 cups boiling water

DIRECTIONS:

1. Generously butter a large baking dish and set the oven to preheat at 350°F with the wire rack in the middle of the oven.

2. In a large bowl, whisk the baking powder and flour to incorporate as much air as possible. Beat in the butter, milk, vanilla, egg, and mashed banana, until you have a lump-free batter. Scrape the batter into the prepared baking dish and smooth it out.

3. In a small glass bowl, whisk together the corn flour and brown sugar before sprinkling it over the batter in an even layer.

4. In a small glass bowl, whisk together the maple syrup, molasses, and boiling water. Carefully ladle the mixture over the pudding.

5. Place the dish in the oven for 30-40 minutes until the top is golden brown and an inserted skewer comes out clean. (Note: The desert may still be jiggly.)

(Tip: Molasses is only low-FODMAP in small servings.)

LOW-FODMAP LEMON MERINGUE TART

COOK TIME: 30 MINS | MAKES: 8-12 SERVINGS

INGREDIENTS:

Pastry:
- ½ tsp. xanthan gum
- 1 ¾ cups gluten-free all-purpose flour
- 8 tbsp. butter, cubed
- 1 tbsp. lactose free milk
- 1 large free-range egg, lightly beaten
- 2 tsp. lactose free milk (for brushing pastry)
- 1 egg yolk (for brushing pastry)

Filling:
- ½ cup granulated white sugar
- 2 large egg yolks

- 2 large eggs
- 4 tsp. lemon rind, grated
- $1/3$ cup lemon juice
- 5 tbsp. butter
- 3 tbsp. corn flour

Topping:
- 4 large egg whites
- 1 ¼ cups icing sugar
- 2 tbsp. corn flour

DIRECTIONS:

1. In a large bowl, whisk together the gum and flour, incorporating as much air as possible. Add the cubed butter to the flour and work it in using your hands until the mixture resembles coarse sand. Use a wooden spoon to stir in the milk and egg until all the pastry ingredients just come together.

2. Use your hands to knead the dough into a ball. Cover the dough in cling wrap and place in the fridge for 30 minutes, or up to 12 hours.

3. Generously butter a 9" pie dish and set the oven to preheat at 350°F with the rack in the lower third of the oven.

4. Place a sheet of greaseproof paper on the counter and roll the dough out to fit the shape of your buttered pie dish. Smooth the sides up and press any breaks back down. Use a fork to liberally prick the base all over.

5. For the pastry brushing; Beat the milk and egg yolk in a small bowl and set aside.

6. Use greaseproof paper to cover the base and fill the dish with uncooked rice. Place the dish in the oven for 5-10 minutes before removing the rice and greaseproof paper and baking for an additional 5 minutes.

7. Remove the dish from the oven and use a basting brush to coat the base with the egg yolk and milk mixture. Return the dish to the oven until the base is nice and browned (approx. 5-10 minutes extra). Allow the base to cool on a wire rack for about 30 minutes, or until cool enough to touch (but not completely cooled) before filling. You may turn off the oven at this point and preheat later on as the following preparations will take a while.

8. For the filling, whisk together the sugar, 2 egg yolks, and 2 whole eggs in a small pot, until velvety. Place the pot over low heat and whisk in the lemon rind, lemon juice, and butter. Whisk throughout for about 5-7 minutes, or until the mixture thickens. Remove the pot from the heat.

9. Whisk the corn flour with ½ cup warm water before adding it to the pot. Whisk for about 2 minutes until the mixture is velvety and thick. Allow the mixture to cool for about 30 minutes.

10. Set the oven to preheat at 325°F.

11. For the topping, use a handheld or stand mixer, beat 4 egg whites until stiff peaks form. Beat in the icing sugar, 1 tbsp. at a time – stop halfway through and beat in the corn flour before adding the rest of the sugar. The egg whites are ready when glossy and stiff peaks form.

12. Scrape the filling into the prepared base and smooth out the top with an offset spatula.

13. Carefully scrape the egg whites onto the filling and smooth out using a clean offset spatula. (Note: You may leave the topping smooth or use a fork to make patterns.)

14. Bake the tart in the oven for 10-15 minutes, or until the peaks are lightly browned. (Note: Keep an eye on the peaks as they can brown quickly.)

15. Allow the tart to cool completely before serving.

STRAWBERRY SCONE TRIFLE

COOK TIME: 15-20 MINS | MAKES: 6 SERVINGS

INGREDIENTS:

- 1 ½ tsp. lemon juice
- ½ cup almond milk
- 1 large free-range egg
- ½ tsp. Kosher salt
- ½ tsp. bicarbonate of soda
- 1 tbsp. baking powder
- 3 tbsp. white sugar
- 1 ½ cups gluten-free all-purpose flour
- ½ cup butter, cubed

- 4 cups strawberries, hulled
- ¼ cup dark brown sugar
- 1 ½ tsp. lemon juice
- 2 tbsp. icing sugar
- 1 ½ cups heavy cream, chilled

DIRECTIONS:

1. Line a baking pan with greaseproof paper and set the oven to preheat at 425°F with the wire rack in the middle of the oven.

2. In a small glass bowl, whisk together the lemon juice and milk and allow the mixture to curdle for 5 minutes before beating in the egg.

3. In a separate bowl, whisk together the salt, bicarbonate of soda, baking powder, white sugar, and flour. Add the butter to the bowl and use 2 sharp knives to "chop" the butter into the flour mixture to form small beads.

4. Stir the egg mixture into the flour until all of the ingredients are just combined. Bring the dough together with your hands before dividing it into 6 equal portions. Shape each portion into a "scone." Place each "scone" onto the prepared baking pan – leave a few inches between each – and bake in the oven for 10-15 minutes. (Note: The "scones" should be baked through and only slightly browned on top.) Allow the "scones" to cool on the pan before using.

5. Roughly chop half of the strawberries and place them in a small pot over medium heat with 3 tbsp. brown sugar. Stir the strawberries for about 5 minutes or until you have a simmering jam that has darkened in color. Transfer the pot to a wooden chopping board and allow the jam to cool.

6. Roughly chop the remaining strawberries and place them in a bowl with the sugar and lemon juice, stirring until properly combined. Allow the bowl to sit on the counter for about 15 minutes until the sugar breaks down – stir at regular intervals. Gently fold the strawberries into the pot of jam.

7. In a large mixing bowl, combine the icing sugar and cream. Beat on high until the cream doubles in size, then beat on low until soft peaks just begin to form – you don't want to overbeat.

8. To build the trifles, halve the "scones" using a sharp knife. Place the bottom halves on the bottom of 6 dessert bowls and top with generous amounts of strawberry jam. Plop the whipped cream on top before placing the top halves of the "scones" on the cream.

9. Allow the trifles to stand for 5 minutes before serving.

ORANGE CHOCOLATE-BOMB COOKIES

COOK TIME: 14 MINS | MAKES: 15 SERVINGS

INGREDIENTS:

- ½ tsp. kosher salt
- 2 tbsp. white sugar
- 2 cups gluten-free pancake mix
- 1 cup lactose free milk
- 1 large free-range egg
- ½ tsp. pure vanilla essence
- ¼ butter, melted
- 2 tsp. orange peel, grated

- ½ cup dark chocolate chips
- 1 cup icing sugar
- 1 tbsp. orange juice

DIRECTIONS:

1. Line a large baking pan with greaseproof paper and set the oven to preheat at 400°F with the wire rack in the middle of the oven.

2. In a large bowl, whisk together the salt, white sugar, and pancake mix. Set aside.

3. In a separate bowl, whisk together the milk and egg before whisking in the vanilla.

4. Beat the milk mixture into the bowl with the flour. Stir in the butter and use your hands to knead the dough before folding in the orange peel and chocolate chips.

5. Use an ice cream scoop to plop 15 cookies onto the prepared baking pan, spacing them evenly apart and then flattening them slightly. Place the pan in the oven until the cookies are golden brown (approx. 12-14 minutes). Allow the cookies to sit outside the oven for 5 minutes.

6. Meanwhile, in a small glass bowl, whisk together the icing sugar and orange juice. When the cookies are cooled, drizzle the glaze over the cookies and serve.

ZESTY LOW-FODMAP LEMON BARS

COOK TIME: 18-30 MINS | MAKES: 16 SERVINGS

INGREDIENTS:

- ¼ tsp. Kosher salt
- 3 tbsp. brown sugar
- ½ cup butter, melted
- 1 cup + 1 tbsp. gluten-free all-purpose flour

Filling:
- 3 tbsp. gluten-free all-purpose flour
- 1 ¼ cup white sugar
- $^2/_3$ cups lemon juice
- 3 large free-range eggs

DIRECTIONS:

1. Line a rimmed baking sheet with greaseproof paper, allowing a few inches to hang over the sides to serve as handles, and set the oven to preheat at 350°F. Make sure the wire rack is placed in the middle of the oven.

2. Whisk the salt, brown sugar, and butter together in a medium bowl. Gently stir in the flour until the mixture just comes together in a batter. Push the batter onto the sheet with the greaseproof paper in an even layer.

3. Place the sheet in the oven until nicely browned (approx. 25 minutes).

4. Whisk the flour and white sugar together in a large bowl.

5. Whisk in the lemon juice until properly combined before beating in the eggs.

6. When the crust is done, remove the sheet from the oven and lower the temperature to 325°F. Scrape the batter onto the browned crust and use an offset spatula to smooth out the surface. Return the sheet to the oven until the filling is no longer jiggly (approx. 18-22 minutes).

7. Allow the bar to cool on a wire rack before slicing into smaller bars and serving. (Note: For an even firmer bar that is easier to slice, chill the bars for 1 hour.)

SAUCE ITSELF CHOCOLATE PUDDING

COOK TIME: 15 MINS | MAKES: 4-6 SERVINGS

INGREDIENTS:

- 2 ½ tbsp. pure cocoa powder
- 2 tsp. baking powder
- ¼ cup dark brown sugar
- 1 tbsp. almond meal
- ½ cup gluten-free all-purpose flour
- 1 tsp. pure vanilla extract
- 1 large free-range egg, lightly beaten
- 2 tbsp. butter, melted
- ½ cup lactose free milk
- 2 oz. dark chocolate, finely chopped
- ¼ cup dark brown sugar
- 1 tbsp. pure cocoa powder
- 1 cup boiling water

DIRECTIONS:

1. Generously butter a large casserole dish and set the oven to preheat at 350°F with the wire rack in the middle of the oven.

2. In a large bowl, whisk together the cocoa powder, baking powder, brown sugar, almond meal, and flour – incorporate as much air as possible. Set aside.

3. Whisk the vanilla, egg, butter, and almond milk together in a separate bowl.

4. Fold the milk mixture into the flour until properly combined and then scrape the batter into your buttered casserole dish. Smooth out the top using an offset spatula before liberally sprinkling the chopped chocolate over the top.

5. In a small glass bowl, whisk together the sugar and cocoa powder before sprinkling it over the chopped chocolate. Carefully ladle the boiling water over the top of the pudding.

6. Place the dish in the oven until an inserted skewer comes out clean (approx. 15 minutes).

LOW-FODMAP STRAWBERRY CHEESECAKE

COOK TIME: 1 HOUR| MAKES: 12-24 SERVINGS

INGREDIENTS:

- 1 ¼ cups crushed gluten-free cookies
- 1-6 tbsp. butter
- 8 oz. lactose-free cream cheese
- 1 tsp. vanilla essence
- 1 tsp. lemon juice
- ¾ cup white sugar
- 5 large free-range eggs, beaten
- 1 cup lactose-free sour cream

Topping:
- 1 lb. fresh strawberries, hulled
- 1 tbsp. lemon juice
- ¼ cup white sugar
- 1 ½ tsp. corn flour
- 1 tbsp. cold water

DIRECTIONS:

1. Set the oven to preheat at 375°F with the wire rack in the middle of the oven.

2. Prepare a large springform cake tin by coating it with baking spray and covering the outside with tin foil in a double layer – fold the edges of the foil over the rims.

3. In a large bowl, use a wooden spoon to combine the crushed cookies with just enough of the butter to moisten them and allow them to come together in a crust. Scrape the moistened cookie crumbs into the prepared cake tin and use the back of a glass to firmly press them down.

4. Place the crust in the oven and bake for 10-12 minutes, or until the crust is nice and browned. Remove the cake tin from the oven and cool on a wire rack. Reduce the oven temperature to 325°F.

5. Beat half of the cream cheese with an electric mixer until light and fluffy. Beat in the vanilla, lemon juice, and sugar. With the mixer running, gradually beat in the beaten eggs. Add the remaining cream cheese and sour cream, beating until everything is just combined. Do not overbeat at this point. (Note: If the mixture seems like it is not coming together properly, use a hand whisk to gently fold it together.) Scrape the batter onto the prepared crust, smoothing out the top.

6. Place the cake tin in an oven-safe casserole dish filled with about 1" boiling water. Place the cake in the oven until the edges are lightly browned and the center is firm (approx. 1 hour). After an hour, turn off the oven but leave the cake in the oven for an additional 20 minutes.

7. Transfer the cake to a wooden chopping board and use a knife that has been dipped in warm water to pry the edges away from the tin (Note: This will ensure that the cake does not crack when being removed later on). Once you have loosened the edges, take the tin out of the water and discard the foil before chilling the cake for up to 48 hours, or overnight.

8. Split the strawberries in half – choose the prettiest ones to garnish the cake and set them apart from the other pile. Take the strawberries that you will not be using for garnish and combine them in a small pot with the lemon juice and sugar. Place the pot over medium heat, crushing the strawberries as you go. Stir for about 3 minutes.

9. In a small glass bowl, whisk together the corn flour and cold water to form a paste. Whisk the paste into the strawberry jam for about 1 minute, or until the jam thickens. Remove the pot from the stove and press the jam through a sieve into a bowl using a wooden spoon or rubber spatula.

10. While the jam cools, remove the cake from the fridge and gently pry open the tin – use a slightly warmed rubber spatula or knife to gently move the cake away from the sides. Place the cake on a platter and use the reserved strawberries to garnish the top. When the jam has cooled, carefully pour it over the strawberries, coating the top of the cake in an even layer.

11. The cheesecake is now ready to serve..

CONCLUSION

I would like to personally thank every single one of you that has purchased this book. It is an immense pleasure to not only gain this knowledge but share it with the world. By making cooking simpler and more enjoyable, we are not only encouraging healthier eating, but also helping the world by discovering more efficient ways to eat and feel better.

I hope you try each and every one of these recipes. Remember with cooking you can adjust the recipes and add substitutes to suit your specific tastes – just keep them low-FODMAP approved.

My goal is for you have fun with your new and improved way of eating, bloat free!

METRIC EQUIVALENCE CHART

Volume Measurements		Weight Measurements		Temperature Conversion	
U.S.	Metric	U.S.	Metric	Fahrenheit	Celsius
1 teaspoon	5 ml	1/2 ounce	15 g	250	120
1 tablespoon	15 ml	1 ounce	30 g	300	150
1/4 cup	60 ml	3 ounces	85 g	325	160
1/3 cup	80 ml	4 ounces	115 g	350	175
1/2 cup	125 ml	8 ounces	225 g	375	190
2/3 cup	160 ml	12 ounces	340 g	400	200
3/4 cup	180 ml	1 pound	450 g	425	220
1 cup	250 ml	2-1/4 pounds	1 kg	450	230

Printed in Great Britain
by Amazon